GREAT

AMERICAN

TREASURE HUNTING

STORIES

LYONS PRESS CLASSICS

GREAT AMERICAN TREASURE HUNTING STORIES

EDITED BY
LAMAR UNDERWOOD

LYONS
PRESS

GUILFORD
CONNECTICUT

An imprint of Globe Pequot, the trade division of
The Rowman & Littlefield Publishing Group, Inc.
4501 Forbes Blvd., Ste. 200
Lanham, MD 20706
www.rowman.com

Distributed by NATIONAL BOOK NETWORK

British Library Cataloguing in Publication Information Available

Library of Congress Cataloging-in-Publication Data
Names: Underwood, Lamar, editor.
Title: Great American treasure hunting stories /
edited by Lamar Underwood.

Description: Guilford, Connecticut : Lyons Press, 2021. | Includes
bibliographical references. | Summary: "A collection of writings about
treasure hunts, edited by Lamar Underwood"—Provided by publisher.
Identifiers: LCCN 2021021706 (print) | LCCN 2021021707 (ebook) | ISBN
9781493035168 (paperback) | ISBN 9781493035175 (epub)
Subjects: LCSH: Treasure hunting—Fiction. | Buried treasure—Fiction.
Classification: LCC PS648.T74 G74 2021 (print) | LCC PS648.T74 (ebook)
DDC 813.008/0353—dc23
LC record available at https://lccn.loc.gov/2021021706
LC ebook record available at https://lccn.loc.gov/2021021707

CONTENTS

INTRODUCTION

Two of mankind's most persistent quests—"get rich quick" and "something for nothing"— provide the power driving these tales of treasure seekers in action. Renowned storytellers like Jack London join real-life adventurers risking their lives for riches they think are worth the dangers.

Buried treasure, creeks glittering with gold nuggets, sunken galleons filled with Spanish doubloons— the mother lodes are as varied as the men pursuing them. Some of the seekers are rewarded; others face tragedy in remote places, lost among the jungles, mountains, and oceans. In both fiction and nonfiction, these stories make treasure hunting a real-life experience, in gripping prose that makes the reader part of the hunt itself.

While it is true that the simple words *treasure hunting* cast a certain spell suggesting glamorous adventure with the possibilities of prodigious riches, the treasure hunts described in these stories reveal truths and difficulties unimagined in the skylarking fantasies that come to the minds of armchair treasure seekers: grueling, backbreaking labor with dangers poised to strike at any moment. Gold seekers and other treasure hunters are true gamblers, risking not only their time and expenses on their searches, but their lives as well.

Most of the stories in this collection take place in two historic episodes that sent hundreds of thousands of men into the wilderness with dreams of striking it rich. The California Gold Rush (1848–1855) and the Klondike Gold Rush (1897–1898). The Klondike pulled over 100,000 prospectors, called "Stampeders," seeking the goldfields around Dawson City, at the juncture of the Klondike and Yukon Rivers.

There were only two ways to reach Dawson City. One was the long route by sea around the Gulf of Alaska, coming into the Yukon from the north, a seemingly impossible journey for most Stampeders. Popular routes involved steamboat trips from ports like Seattle to reach southeast Alaska, where men then made their way overland to the Klondike, a territory of Canada's northwest, in British domain. The drama of immense difficulties loomed for the prospectors as they tried to reach the Chilkoot Trail out of Dyea or the White Pass Trail out of Skagway. With the equipment needed and the terrain traversed, it required many weeks, even months, to reach Dawson. Failures were rampart; suicides and murder were common. The difficulties and tragedies of the journeys are described in these pages.

California and the Klondike provided the settings and activities for many of the intrepid treasure hunters to put pen to paper and capture the drama of those days in published works. Well-known writers like Jack London, Bret Harte, Mark Twain, and Rex Beach added their names to the avalanche of treasure-hunting literature composed mostly of unknown authors who were not professional writers but could not resist sharing the stories of adventures far beyond the lives of ordinary citizens.

Citizens who, like this editor and our readers, must experience the great adventures that appeal to us in print.

Editor's note: misspellings and errors in punctuation have not been corrected from the original texts.

1

ALL GOLD CANYON

BY JACK LONDON

Color!

As the water sloshes over the sand at the bottom of the prospector's pan, the swirling motions reveal a breathtaking sight: color! There's not much—only a hint of golden hue—but that's enough. This is the place! Here among the lonely mountains and forested slopes, the tiny stream has given up the first hints of treasure.

Now the work begins. In the hours and days ahead, the prospector will learn if this is a true strike, or merely a tease. Packing supplies on his horse, the prospector is prepared to explore the possibilities of this site as long as his enthusiasm holds out. This is the Yukon in 1897 and dreams of treasure have brought many men to these remote hills and streams.

Among all Jack London's tales of outdoor adventure, "All Gold Canyon" is one of the two best you'll find that make you, the reader, part of the story—alone in the wilds, counting on your experience and skills to strike it rich. The other? It's "To Build a Fire," a survival story (see chapter 7).

Haven't you always wanted to go prospecting? Dip your pan into untouched streams of pure mountain water? No crowds, no pushing.

Well, here's what it's like. And even though you don't realize it, there's danger ahead.

It was the green heart of the canyon, where the walls swerved back from the rigid plan and relieved their harshness of line by making a little sheltered nook and filling it to the brim with sweetness and roundness and softness. Here all things rested. Even the narrow stream ceased its turbulent down-rush long enough to form a quiet pool. Knee-deep in the water, with drooping head and half-shut eyes, drowsed a red-coated, many-antlered buck.

On one side, beginning at the very lip of the pool, was a tiny meadow, a cool, resilient surface of green that extended to the base of the frowning wall. Beyond the pool a gentle slope of earth ran up and up to meet the opposing wall. Fine grass covered the slope— grass that was spangled with flowers, with here and there patches of color, orange and purple and golden. Below, the canyon was shut in. There was no view. The walls leaned together abruptly and the canyon ended in a chaos of rocks, moss-covered and hidden by a green screen of vines and creepers and boughs of trees. Up the canyon rose far hills and peaks, the big foothills, pine-covered and remote. And far beyond, like clouds upon the border of the slay, towered minarets of white, where the Sierra's eternal snows flashed austerely the blazes of the sun.

There was no dust in the canyon. The leaves and flowers were clean and virginal. The grass was young velvet. Over the pool three cotton-woods sent their scurvy fluffs fluttering down the quiet air. On the slope the blossoms of the wine-wooded manzanita filled the air with springtime odors, while the leaves, wise with experience, were already beginning their vertical twist against the coming aridity of summer. In the open spaces on the slope, beyond the farthest shadow-reach of the manzanita, poised the mariposa lilies, like so many flights of jewelled moths suddenly arrested and on the verge of trembling into flight again. Here and there that woods harlequin, the madrone, permitting itself to be caught in the act of changing its pea-green trunk to madder-red, breathed its fragrance into the air from great clusters of waxen bells. Creamy white were these bells, shaped like lilies-of-the-valley, with the sweetness of perfume that is of the springtime.

There was not a sigh of wind. The air was drowsy with its weight of perfume. It was a sweetness that would have been cloying had the air been heavy and humid. But the air was sharp and thin. It was as starlight transmuted into atmosphere, shot through and warmed by sunshine, and flower-drenched with sweetness.

An occasional butterfly drifted in and out through the patches of light and shade. And from all about rose the low and sleepy hum of mountain bees—feasting Sybarites that jostled one another good-naturedly at the board, nor found time for rough discourtesy. So quietly did the little stream drip and ripple its way through the canyon that it spoke only in faint and occasional gurgles. The voice of the stream was as a drowsy whisper, ever interrupted by dozings and silences, ever lifted again in the awakenings.

The motion of all things was a drifting in the heart of the canyon. Sunshine and butterflies drifted in and out among the trees. The hum of the bees and the whisper of the stream were a drifting of sound. And the drifting sound and drifting color seemed to weave together in the making of a delicate and intangible fabric which was the spirit of the place. It was a spirit of peace that was not of death, but of smooth-pulsing life, of quietude that was not silence, of movement that was not action, of repose that was quick with existence without being violent with struggle and travail. The spirit of the place was the spirit of the peace of the living, somnolent with the easement and content of prosperity, and undisturbed by rumors of far wars.

The red-coated, many-antlered buck acknowledged the lordship of the spirit of the place and dozed knee-deep in the cool, shaded pool.

There seemed no flies to vex him and he was languid with rest. Sometimes his ears moved when the stream awoke and whispered; but they moved lazily, with foreknowledge that it was merely the stream grown garrulous at discovery that it had slept.

But there came a time when the buck's ears lifted and tensed with swift eagerness for sound. His head was turned down the canyon. His sensitive, quivering nostrils scented the air. His eyes could not pierce the green screen through which the stream rippled away, but to his ears came the voice of a man. It was a steady, monotonous, singsong voice. Once the buck heard the harsh clash of metal upon rock. At the sound he snorted with a sudden start that jerked him through the air from water to meadow, and his feet sank into the young velvet, while he pricked his ears and again scented the air. Then he stole across the tiny meadow, pausing once and again to listen, and faded away out of the canyon like a wraith, soft-footed and without sound.

The clash of steel-shod soles against the rocks began to be heard, and the man's voice grew louder. It was raised in a sort of chant and became distinct with nearness, so that the words could be heard:

> Tu'n around an' tu'n yo' face
> Untoe them sweet hills of grace
> (D' pow'rs of sin yo' am scornin'!).
> Look about an, look aroun',
> Fling yo' sin-pack on d' groun'
> (Yo' will meet wid d' Lord in d' mornin'!).

A sound of scrambling accompanied the song, and the spirit of the place fled away on the heels of the red-coated buck. The green screen was burst asunder, and a man peered out at the meadow and the pool and the sloping side-hill. He was a deliberate sort of man. He took in the scene with one embracing glance, then ran his eyes over the details to verify the general impression. Then, and not until then, did he open his mouth in vivid and solemn approval:

"Smoke of life an' snakes of purgatory! Will you just look at that! Wood an' water an' grass an' a side-hill! A pocket-hunter's delight an' a cayuse's paradise! Cool green for tired eyes! Pink pills for pale people ain't in it. A secret pasture for prospectors and a resting-place for tired burros, by damn!"

He was a sandy-complexioned man in whose face geniality and humor seemed the salient characteristics. It was a mobile face, quick-changing to inward mood and thought. Thinking was in him a visible process. Ideas chased across his face like wind-flaws across the surface of a lake. His hair, sparse and unkempt of growth, was as indeterminate and colorless as his complexion. It would seem that all the color of his frame had gone into his eyes, for they were startlingly blue. Also, they were laughing and merry eyes, within them much of the naivete and wonder of the child; and yet, in an unassertive way, they contained much of calm self-reliance and strength of purpose founded upon self-experience and experience of the world.

From out the screen of vines and creepers he flung ahead of him a miner's pick and shovel and gold-pan. Then he crawled out himself into the open. He was clad in faded overalls and black cotton shirt, with hobnailed brogans on his feet, and on his head a hat whose shapelessness and stains advertised the rough usage of wind and rain and sun and camp-smoke. He stood erect, seeing wide-eyed the secrecy of the scene and sensuously inhaling the warm, sweet breath of the canyon-garden through nostrils that dilated and quivered with delight. His eyes narrowed to laughing slits of blue, his face wreathed itself in joy, and his mouth curled in a smile as he cried aloud:

"Jumping dandelions and happy hollyhocks, but that smells good to me! Talk about your attar o' roses an' cologne factories! They ain't in it!"

He had the habit of soliloquy. His quick-changing facial expressions might tell every thought and mood, but the tongue, perforce, ran hard after, repeating, like a second Boswell.

The man lay down on the lip of the pool and drank long and deep of its water. "Tastes good to me," he murmured, lifting his head and gazing across the pool at the side-hill, while he wiped his mouth with the back of his hand. The side-hill attracted his attention. Still lying on his stomach, he studied the hill formation long and carefully. It was a practised eye that travelled up the slope to the crumbling canyon-wall and back and down again to the edge of the pool. He scrambled to his feet and favored the side-hill with a second survey.

"Looks good to me," he concluded, picking up his pick and shovel and gold-pan.

He crossed the stream below the pool, stepping agilely from stone to stone. Where the sidehill touched the water he dug up a shovelful of dirt and put it into the gold-pan. He squatted down, holding the pan in his two hands, and partly immersing it in the stream. Then he imparted to the pan a deft circular motion that sent the water sluicing in and out through the dirt and gravel. The larger and the lighter particles worked to the surface, and these, by a skilful dipping movement of the pan, he spilled out and over the edge. Occasionally, to expedite matters, he rested the pan and with his fingers raked out the large pebbles and pieces of rock.

The contents of the pan diminished rapidly until only fine dirt and the smallest bits of gravel remained. At this stage he began to work very deliberately and carefully. It was fine washing, and he washed fine and finer, with a keen scrutiny and delicate and fastidious touch. At last the pan seemed empty of everything but water; but with a quick semicircular flirt that sent the water flying over the shallow rim into the stream, he disclosed a layer of black sand on the bottom of the pan. So thin was this layer that it was like a streak of paint. He examined it closely. In the midst of it was a tiny golden speck. He dribbled a little water in over the depressed edge of the pan. With a quick flirt he sent the water sluicing across the bottom, turning the grains of black sand over and over. A second tiny golden speck rewarded his effort.

The washing had now become very fine—fine beyond all need of ordinary placer-mining. He worked the black sand, a small portion at a time, up the shallow rim of the pan. Each small portion he examined sharply, so that his eyes saw every grain of it before he allowed it to slide over the edge and away. Jealously, bit by bit, he let the black sand slip away. A golden speck, no larger than a pin-point, appeared on the rim, and by his manipulation of the riveter it returned to the bottom of the pan. And in such fashion another speck was disclosed, and another. Great was his care of them. Like a shepherd he herded his flock of golden specks so that not one should be lost. At last, of the pan of dirt nothing remained but his golden herd. He counted it, and then, after all his labor, sent it flying out of the pan with one final swirl of water.

But his blue eyes were shining with desire as he rose to his feet. "Seven," he muttered aloud, asserting the sum of the specks for which he had toiled so hard and which he had so wantonly thrown away. "Seven," he repeated, with the emphasis of one trying to impress a number on his memory.

He stood still a long while, surveying the hill-side. In his eyes was a curiosity, new-aroused and burning. There was an exultance about his bearing and a keenness like that of a hunting animal catching the fresh scent of game.

He moved down the stream a few steps and took a second panful of dirt.

Again came the careful washing, the jealous herding of the golden specks, and the wantonness with which he sent them flying into the stream when he had counted their number.

"Five," he muttered, and repeated, "five."

He could not forbear another survey of the hill before filling the pan farther down the stream. His golden herds diminished. "Four, three, two, two, one," were his memory-tabulations as he moved down the stream. When but one speck of gold rewarded his washing, he stopped and built a fire of dry twigs. Into this he thrust the gold-pan and burned it till it was blue-black. He held up the pan and examined it critically. Then he nodded approbation. Against such a color-background he could defy the tiniest yellow speck to elude him.

Still moving down the stream, he panned again. A single speck was his reward. A third pan contained no gold at all. Not satisfied with this, he panned three times again, taking his shovels of dirt within a foot of one another. Each pan proved empty of gold, and the fact, instead of discouraging him, seemed to give him satisfaction. His elation increased with each barren washing, until he arose, exclaiming jubilantly:

"If it ain't the real thing, may God knock off my head with sour apples!"

Returning to where he had started operations, he began to pan up the stream. At first his golden herds increased—increased prodigiously. "Fourteen, eighteen, twenty-one, twenty-six," ran his memory tabulations. Just above the pool he struck his richest pan—thirty-five colors.

"Almost enough to save," he remarked regretfully as he allowed the water to sweep them away.

The sun climbed to the top of the sky. The man worked on. Pan by pan, he went up the stream, the tally of results steadily decreasing.

"It's just booful, the way it peters out," he exulted when a shovelful of dirt contained no more than a single speck of gold.

And when no specks at all were found in several pans, he straightened up and favored the hillside with a confident glance.

"Ah, ha! Mr. Pocket!" he cried out, as though to an auditor hidden somewhere above him beneath the surface of the slope. "Ah, ha! Mr. Pocket! I'm a-comin', I'm a-comin', an' I'm shorely gwine to get yer! You heah me, Mr. Pocket? I'm gwine to get yer as shore as punkins ain't cauliflowers!"

He turned and flung a measuring glance at the sun poised above him in the azure of the cloudless sky. Then he went down the canyon, following the line of shovel-holes he had made in filling the pans. He crossed the stream below the pool and disappeared through the green screen. There was little opportunity for the spirit of the place to return with its quietude and repose, for the man's voice, raised in ragtime song, still dominated the canyon with possession.

After a time, with a greater clashing of steel-shod feet on rock, he returned. The green screen was tremendously agitated. It surged back and forth in the throes of a struggle. There was a loud grating and clanging of metal. The man's voice leaped to a higher pitch and was sharp with imperativeness. A large body plunged and panted. There was a snapping and ripping and rending, and amid a shower of falling leaves a horse burst through the screen. On its back was a pack, and from this trailed broken vines and torn creepers. The animal gazed with astonished eyes at the scene into which it had been precipitated, then dropped its head to the grass and began contentedly to graze. A second horse scrambled into view, slipping once on the mossy rocks and regaining equilibrium when its hoofs sank into the yielding surface of the meadow. It was riderless, though on its back was a high-horned Mexican saddle, scarred and discolored by long usage.

The man brought up the rear. He threw off pack and saddle, with an eye to camp location, and gave the animals their freedom to graze. He unpacked his food and got out frying-pan and coffee-pot. He gathered an armful of dry wood, and with a few stones made a place for his fire.

"My!" he said, "but I've got an appetite. I could scoff iron-filings an' horseshoe nails an' thank you kindly, ma'am, for a second helpin'."

He straightened up, and, while he reached for matches in the pocket of his overalls, his eyes travelled across the pool to the side-hill. His fingers had clutched the match-box, but they relaxed their hold and the hand came out empty. The man wavered perceptibly. He looked at his preparations for cooking and he looked at the hill.

"Guess I'll take another whack at her," he concluded, starting to cross the stream.

"They ain't no sense in it, I know," he mumbled apologetically. "But keepin' grub back an hour ain't goin' to hurt none, I reckon."

A few feet back from his first line of test-pans he started a second line. The sun dropped down the western sky, the shadows lengthened, but the man worked on. He began a third line of test-pans. He was cross-cutting the hillside, line by line, as he ascended. The centre of each line produced the richest pans, while the ends came where no colors showed in the pan. And as he ascended the hillside the lines grew perceptibly shorter. The regularity with which their length diminished served to indicate that somewhere up the slope the last line would be so short as to have scarcely length at all, and that beyond could come only a point. The design was growing into an inverted "V." The converging sides of this "V" marked the boundaries of the gold-bearing dirt.

The apex of the "V" was evidently the man's goal. Often he ran his eye along the converging sides and on up the hill, trying to divine the apex, the point where the gold-bearing dirt must cease. Here resided "Mr. Pocket"—for so the man familiarly addressed the imaginary point above him on the slope, crying out:

"Come down out o' that, Mr. Pocket! Be right smart an' agreeable, an' come down!"

"All right," he would add later, in a voice resigned to determination. "All right, Mr. Pocket. It's plain to me I got to come right up an' snatch you out bald-headed. An' I'll do it! I'll do it!" he would threaten still later.

Each pan he carried down to the water to wash, and as he went higher up the hill the pans grew richer, until he began to save the gold in an empty baking-powder can which he carried carelessly in his hip-pocket. So engrossed was he in his toil that he did not notice the long twilight of oncoming night. It was not until he tried vainly to see the gold colors in the bottom of the pan that he realized the passage of time. He straightened up abruptly. An expression of whimsical wonderment and awe overspread his face as he drawled:

"Gosh darn my buttons! if I didn't plumb forget dinner!"

He stumbled across the stream in the darkness and lighted his long-delayed fire. Flapjacks and bacon and warmed-over beans constituted his supper. Then he smoked a pipe by the smouldering coals, listening to the night noises and watching the moonlight stream through the canyon. After that he unrolled his bed, took off his heavy shoes, and pulled the blankets up to his chin. His face showed white in the moonlight, like the face of a corpse. But it was a corpse that knew its resurrection, for the man rose suddenly on one elbow and gazed across at his hillside.

"Good night, Mr. Pocket," he called sleepily. "Good night."

He slept through the early gray of morning until the direct rays of the sun smote his closed eyelids, when he awoke with a start and looked about him until he had established the continuity of his existence and identified his present self with the days previously lived.

To dress, he had merely to buckle on his shoes. He glanced at his fireplace and at his hillside, wavered, but fought down the temptation and started the fire.

"Keep yer shirt on, Bill; keep yer shirt on," he admonished himself. "What's the good of rushin'? No use in gettin' all het up an' sweaty. Mr. Pocket'll wait for you. He ain't a-runnin' away before you can get yer breakfast. Now, what you want, Bill, is something fresh in yer bill o' fare. So it's up to you to go an' get it."

He cut a short pole at the water's edge and drew from one of his pockets a bit of line and a draggled fly that had once been a royal coachman.

"Mebbe they'll bite in the early morning," he muttered, as he made his first cast into the pool. And a moment later he was gleefully crying: "What'd I tell you, eh? What'd I tell you?"

He had no reel, nor any inclination to waste time, and by main strength, and swiftly, he drew out of the water a flashing ten-inch trout. Three more, caught in rapid succession, furnished his breakfast. When he came to the stepping-stones on his way to his hillside, he was struck by a sudden thought, and paused.

"I'd just better take a hike down-stream a ways," he said. "There's no tellin' what cuss may be snoopin' around."

But he crossed over on the stones, and with a "I really oughter take that hike," the need of the precaution passed out of his mind and he fell to work.

At nightfall he straightened up. The small of his back was stiff from stooping toil, and as he put his hand behind him to soothe the protesting muscles, he said:

"Now what d'ye think of that, by damn? I clean forgot my dinner again! If I don't watch out, I'll sure be degeneratin' into a two-meal-a-day crank."

"Pockets is the damnedest things I ever see for makin' a man absent-minded," he communed that night, as he crawled into his blankets. Nor did he forget to call up the hillside, "Good night, Mr. Pocket! Good night!"

Rising with the sun, and snatching a hasty breakfast, he was early at work. A fever seemed to be growing in him, nor did the increasing richness of the test-pans allay this fever. There was a flush in his cheek other than that made by the heat of the sun, and he was oblivious to fatigue and the passage of time. When he filled a pan with dirt, he ran down the hill to wash it; nor could he forbear running up the hill again, panting and stumbling profanely, to refill the pan.

He was now a hundred yards from the water, and the inverted "V" was assuming definite proportions. The width of the pay-dirt steadily decreased, and the man extended in his mind's eye the sides of the "V" to their meeting-place far up the hill. This was his goal, the apex of the "V," and he panned many times to locate it.

"Just about two yards above that manzanita bush an' a yard to the right," he finally concluded.

Then the temptation seized him. "As plain as the nose on your face," he said, as he abandoned his laborious cross-cutting and climbed to the indicated apex. He filled a pan and carried it down the hill to wash. It contained no trace of gold. He dug deep, and he dug shallow, filling and washing a dozen pans, and was unrewarded even by the tiniest golden speck. He was enraged at having yielded to the temptation, and cursed himself blasphemously and pridelessly. Then he went down the hill and took up the cross-cutting.

"Slow an' certain, Bill; slow an' certain," he crooned. "Short-cuts to fortune ain't in your line, an' it's about time you know it. Get wise, Bill; get wise. Slow an' certain's the only hand you can play; so go to it, an' keep to it, too."

As the cross-cuts decreased, showing that the sides of the "V" were converging, the depth of the "V" increased. The gold-trace was dipping into the hill. It was only at thirty inches beneath the surface that he could get colors in his pan. The dirt he found at twenty-five inches from the surface, and at thirty-five inches, yielded barren pans. At the base of the "V," by the water's edge, he had found the gold colors at the grass roots. The higher he went up the hill, the deeper the gold dipped.

To dig a hole three feet deep in order to get one test-pan was a task of no mean magnitude; while between the man and the apex intervened an untold number of such holes to be. "An' there's no tellin' how much deeper it'll pitch," he sighed, in a moment's pause, while his fingers soothed his aching back.

Feverish with desire, with aching back and stiffening muscles, with pick and shovel gouging and mauling the soft brown earth, the man toiled up the hill. Before him was the smooth slope, spangled with flowers and made sweet with their breath. Behind him was devastation. It looked like some terrible eruption breaking out on the smooth skin of the hill. His slow progress was like that of a slug, befouling beauty with a monstrous trail.

Though the dipping gold-trace increased the man's work, he found consolation in the increasing richness of the pans. Twenty cents, thirty cents, fifty cents, sixty cents, were the values of the gold found in the pans, and at nightfall he washed his banner pan, which gave him a dollar's worth of gold-dust from a shovelful of dirt.

"I'll just bet it's my luck to have some inquisitive cuss come buttin' in here on my pasture," he mumbled sleepily that night as he pulled the blankets up to his chin.

Suddenly he sat upright. "Bill!" he called sharply. "Now, listen to me, Bill; d'ye hear! It's up to you, to-morrow mornin', to mosey round an' see what you can see. Understand? Tomorrow morning, an' don't you forget it!"

He yawned and glanced across at his side-hill. "Good night, Mr. Pocket," he called.

In the morning he stole a march on the sun, for he had finished breakfast when its first rays caught him, and he was climbing the wall of the canyon where it crumbled away and gave footing. From the outlook at the top he found himself in the midst of loneliness. As far as he could see, chain after chain of mountains heaved themselves into his vision. To the east his eyes, leaping the miles between range and range and between many ranges, brought up at last against the white-peaked Sierras—the main crest, where the backbone of the Western world reared itself against the sky. To the north and south he could see more distinctly the cross-systems that broke through the main trend of the sea of mountains. To the west the ranges fell away, one behind the other, diminishing and fading into the gentle foothills that, in turn, descended into the great valley which he could not see.

And in all that mighty sweep of earth he saw no sign of man nor of the handiwork of man—save only the torn bosom of the hillside at his feet. The man looked long and carefully. Once, far down his own canyon, he thought he saw in the air a faint hint of smoke. He looked again and decided that it was the purple haze of the hills made dark by a convolution of the canyon wall at its back.

"Hey, you, Mr. Pocket!" he called down into the canyon. "Stand out from under! I'm a-comin', Mr. Pocket! I'm a-comin'!"

The heavy brogans on the man's feet made him appear clumsy-footed, but he swung down from the giddy height as lightly and airily as a mountain goat. A rock, turning under his foot on the edge of the precipice, did not disconcert him. He seemed to know the precise time required for the turn to culminate in disaster, and in the meantime he utilized the false footing itself for the momentary earth-contact necessary to carry him on into safety. Where the earth sloped so steeply that it was impossible to stand for a second upright, the man did not hesitate. His foot pressed the impossible surface for but a fraction of the fatal second and gave him the bound that carried him onward. Again, where even the fraction of a second's footing was out of the question, he would swing his body past by a moment's hand-grip on a jutting knob of rock, a crevice, or a precariously rooted shrub. At last, with a wild leap and yell, he exchanged the face of the wall for an earth-slide and finished the descent in the midst of several tons of sliding earth and gravel.

His first pan of the morning washed out over two dollars in coarse gold. It was from the centre of the "V." To either side the diminution in the values of the pans was swift. His lines of crosscutting holes were growing very short. The converging sides of the inverted "V" were only a few yards apart. Their meeting-point was only a few yards above him. But the pay-streak was dipping deeper and deeper into the earth. By early afternoon he was sinking the test-holes five feet before the pans could show the gold-trace.

For that matter, the gold-trace had become something more than a trace; it was a placer mine in itself, and the man resolved to come back after he had found the pocket and work over the ground. But the increasing richness of the pans began to worry him. By late afternoon the worth of the pans had grown to three and four dollars. The man scratched his head perplexedly and looked a few feet up the hill at the manzanita bush that marked approximately the apex of the "V." He nodded his head and said oracularly:

"It's one o' two things, Bill; one o' two things. Either Mr. Pocket's spilled himself all out an' down the hill, or else Mr. Pocket's that damned rich you maybe won't be able to carry him all away with you. And that'd be hell, wouldn't it, now?" He chuckled at contemplation of so pleasant a dilemma.

Nightfall found him by the edge of the stream, his eyes wrestling with the gathering darkness over the washing of a five-dollar pan.

"Wisht I had an electric light to go on working," he said.

He found sleep difficult that night. Many times he composed himself and closed his eyes for slumber to overtake him; but his blood pounded with too strong desire, and as many times his eyes opened and he murmured wearily, "Wisht it was sun-up."

Sleep came to him in the end, but his eyes were open with the first paling of the stars, and the gray of dawn caught him with breakfast finished and climbing the hillside in the direction of the secret abiding-place of Mr. Pocket.

The first cross-cut the man made, there was space for only three holes, so narrow had become the pay-streak and so close was he to the fountainhead of the golden stream he had been following for four days.

"Be ca'm, Bill; be ca'm," he admonished himself, as he broke ground for the final hole where the sides of the "V" had at last come together in a point.

"I've got the almighty cinch on you, Mr. Pocket, an' you can't lose me," he said many times as he sank the hole deeper and deeper.

Four feet, five feet, six feet, he dug his way down into the earth. The digging grew harder. His pick grated on broken rock. He examined the rock. "Rotten quartz," was his conclusion as, with the shovel, he cleared the bottom of the hole of loose dirt. He attacked the crumbling quartz with the pick, bursting the disintegrating rock asunder with every stroke.

He thrust his shovel into the loose mass. His eye caught a gleam of yellow. He dropped the shovel and squatted suddenly on his heels. As a farmer rubs the clinging earth from fresh-dug potatoes, so the man, a piece of rotten quartz held in both hands, rubbed the dirt away.

"Sufferin' Sardanopolis!" he cried. "Lumps an' chunks of it! Lumps an' chunks of it!"

It was only half rock he held in his hand. The other half was virgin gold. He dropped it into his pan and examined another piece. Little yellow was to be seen, but with his strong fingers he crumbled the rotten quartz away till both hands were filled with glowing yellow. He rubbed the dirt away from fragment after fragment, tossing them into the gold-pan. It was a treasure-hole. So much had the quartz rotted away that there was less of it than there was of gold. Now and again he found a piece to which no rock clung—a piece that was all gold. A chunk, where the pick had laid open the heart of the gold, glittered like a handful of yellow jewels, and he cocked his head at it and slowly turned it around and over to observe the rich play of the light upon it.

"Talk about yer Too Much Gold diggin's!" the man snorted contemptuously. "Why, this diggin' 'd make it look like thirty cents. This diggin' is All Gold. An' right here an' now I name this yere canyon 'All Gold Canyon,' b' gosh!"

Still squatting on his heels, he continued examining the fragments and tossing them into the pan. Suddenly there came to him a premonition of danger. It seemed a shadow had fallen upon him. But there was no shadow. His heart had given a great jump up into his throat and was choking him. Then his blood slowly chilled and he felt the sweat of his shirt cold against his flesh.

He did not spring up nor look around. He did not move. He was considering the nature of the premonition he had received, trying to locate the source of the mysterious force that had warned him, striving to sense the imperative presence of the unseen thing that threatened him. There is an aura of things hostile, made manifest by messengers refined for the senses to know; and this aura he felt, but knew not how he felt it. His was the feeling as when a cloud passes over the sun. It seemed that between him and life had passed something dark and smothering and menacing; a gloom, as it were, that swallowed up life and made for death—his death.

Every force of his being impelled him to spring up and confront the unseen danger, but his soul dominated the panic, and he remained squatting on his heels, in his hands a chunk of gold. He did not dare to look around, but he knew by now that there was something behind him and above him. He made believe to be interested in the gold in his hand. He examined it critically, turned it over and over, and rubbed the dirt from it. And all the time he knew that something behind him was looking at the gold over his shoulder.

Still feigning interest in the chunk of gold in his hand, he listened intently and he heard the breathing of the thing behind him. His eyes searched the ground in front of him for a weapon, but they saw only the uprooted gold, worthless to him now in his extremity. There was his pick, a handy weapon on occasion; but this was not such an occasion. The man realized his predicament. He was in a narrow hole that was seven feet deep. His head did not come to the surface of the ground. He was in a trap.

He remained squatting on his heels. He was quite cool and collected; but his mind, considering every factor, showed him only his helplessness. He continued rubbing the dirt from the quartz fragments and throwing the gold into the pan. There was nothing else for him to do. Yet he knew that he would have to rise up, sooner or later, and face the danger that breathed at his back.

The minutes passed, and with the passage of each minute he knew that by so much he was nearer the time when he must stand up, or else—and his wet shirt went cold against his flesh again at the thought—or else he might receive death as he stooped there over his treasure.

Still he squatted on his heels, rubbing dirt from gold and debating in just what manner he should rise up. He might rise up with a rush and claw his way out of the hole to meet whatever threatened on the even footing above ground. Or he might rise up slowly and carelessly, and feign casually to discover the thing that breathed at his back. His instinct and every fighting fibre of his body favored the mad, clawing rush to the surface. His intellect, and the craft thereof, favored the slow and cautious meeting with the thing that menaced and which he could not see. And while he debated, a loud, crashing noise burst on his ear. At the same instant he received a stunning blow on the left side of the back, and from the point of impact felt a rush of flame through his flesh. He sprang up in the air, but halfway to his feet collapsed. His body crumpled in like a leaf withered in sudden heat, and he came down, his chest across his pan of gold, his face in the dirt and rock, his legs tangled and twisted because of the restricted space at the bottom of the hole. His legs twitched convulsively several times. His body was shaken as with a mighty ague. There was a slow expansion of the lungs, accompanied by a deep sigh. Then the air was slowly, very slowly, exhaled, and his body as slowly flattened itself down into inertness.

Above, revolver in hand, a man was peering down over the edge of the hole. He peered for a long time at the prone and motionless body beneath him. After a while the stranger sat down on the edge of the hole so that he could see into it, and rested the revolver on his knee. Reaching his hand into a pocket, he drew out a wisp of brown paper. Into this he dropped a few crumbs of tobacco. The combination became a cigarette, brown and squat, with the ends turned in. Not once did he take his eyes from the body at the bottom of the hole. He lighted the cigarette and drew its smoke into his lungs with a caressing intake of the breath. He smoked slowly. Once the cigarette went out and he relighted it. And all the while he studied the body beneath him.

In the end he tossed the cigarette stub away and rose to his feet. He moved to the edge of the hole. Spanning it, a hand resting on each edge, and with the revolver still in the right hand, he muscled his body down into the hole. While his feet were yet a yard from the bottom he released his hands and dropped down.

At the instant his feet struck bottom he saw the pocket-miner's arm leap out, and his own legs knew a swift, jerking grip that overthrew him. In the nature of the jump his revolver-hand was above his head. Swiftly as the grip had flashed about his legs, just as swiftly he brought the revolver down. He was still in the air, his fall in process of completion, when he pulled the trigger. The explosion was deafening in the confined space. The smoke filled the hole so that he could see nothing. He struck the bottom on his back, and like a cat's the pocket-miner's body was on top of him. Even as the miner's body passed on top, the stranger crooked in his right arm to fire; and even in that instant the miner, with a quick thrust of elbow, struck his wrist. The muzzle was thrown up and the bullet thudded into the dirt of the side of the hole.

The next instant the stranger felt the miner's hand grip his wrist. The struggle was now for the revolver. Each man strove to turn it against the other's body. The smoke in the hole was clearing. The stranger, lying on his back, was beginning to see dimly. But suddenly he was blinded by a handful of dirt deliberately flung into his eyes by his antagonist. In that moment of shock his grip on the revolver was broken. In the next moment he felt a smashing darkness descend upon his brain, and in the midst of the darkness even the darkness ceased.

But the pocket-miner fired again and again, until the revolver was empty. Then he tossed it from him and, breathing heavily, sat down on the dead man's legs.

The miner was sobbing and struggling for breath. "Measly skunk!" he panted; "a-campin' on my trail an' lettin' me do the work, an' then shootin' me in the back!"

He was half crying from anger and exhaustion. He peered at the face of the dead man. It was sprinkled with loose dirt and gravel, and it was difficult to distinguish the features.

"Never laid eyes on him before," the miner concluded his scrutiny. "Just a common an' ordinary thief, damn him! An' he shot me in the back! He shot me in the back!"

He opened his shirt and felt himself, front and back, on his left side.

"Went clean through, and no harm done!" he cried jubilantly. "I'll bet he aimed right all right, but he drew the gun over when he pulled the trigger—the cuss! But I fixed 'm! Oh, I fixed 'm!"

His fingers were investigating the bullet-hole in his side, and a shade of regret passed over his face. "It's goin' to be stiffer'n hell," he said. "An' it's up to me to get mended an' get out o' here."

He crawled out of the hole and went down the hill to his camp. Half an hour later he returned, leading his pack-horse. His open shirt disclosed the rude bandages with which he had dressed his wound. He was slow and awkward with his left-hand movements, but that did not prevent his using the arm.

The bight of the pack-rope under the dead man's shoulders enabled him to heave the body out of the hole. Then he set to work gathering up his gold. He worked steadily for several hours, pausing often to rest his stiffening shoulder and to exclaim:

"He shot me in the back, the measly skunk! He shot me in the back!"

When his treasure was quite cleaned up and wrapped securely into a number of blanket-covered parcels, he made an estimate of its value.

"Four hundred pounds, or I'm a Hottentot," he concluded. "Say two hundred in quartz an' dirt—that leaves two hundred pounds of gold. Bill! Wake up! Two hundred pounds of gold! Forty thousand dollars! An' it's yourn—all yourn!"

He scratched his head delightedly and his fingers blundered into an unfamiliar groove. They quested along it for several inches. It was a crease through his scalp where the second bullet had ploughed.

He walked angrily over to the dead man.

"You would, would you?" he bullied. "You would, eh? Well, I fixed you good an' plenty, an' I'll give you decent burial, too. That's more'n you'd have done for me."

He dragged the body to the edge of the hole and toppled it in. It struck the bottom with a dull crash, on its side, the face twisted up to the light. The miner peered down at it.

"An' you shot me in the back!" he said accusingly.

With pick and shovel he filled the hole. Then he loaded the gold on his horse. It was too great a load for the animal, and when he had gained his camp he transferred part of it to his saddle-horse. Even so, he was compelled to abandon a portion of his outfit—pick and shovel and gold-pan, extra food and cooking utensils, and divers odds and ends.

The sun was at the zenith when the man forced the horses at the screen of vines and creepers. To climb the huge boulders the animals were compelled to uprear and struggle blindly through the tangled mass of vegetation. Once the saddle-horse fell heavily and the man removed the pack to get the animal on its feet. After it started on its way again the man thrust his head out from among the leaves and peered up at the hillside.

"The measly skunk!" he said, and disappeared.

There was a ripping and tearing of vines and boughs. The trees surged back and forth, marking the passage of the animals through the midst of them. There was a clashing of steel-shod hoofs on stone, and now and again an oath or a sharp cry of command. Then the voice of the man was raised in song:—

> Tu'n around an' tu'n yo' face
> Untoe them sweet hills of grace
> (D' pow'rs of sin yo' am scornin'!).
> Look about an, look aroun',
> Fling yo' sin-pack on d' groun'
> (Yo' will meet wid d' Lord in d' mornin'!).

The song grew faint and fainter, and through the silence crept back the spirit of the place. The stream once more drowsed and whispered; the hum of the mountain bees rose sleepily. Down through the perfume-weighted air fluttered the snowy fluffs of the cottonwoods. The butterflies drifted in and out among the trees, and over all blazed the quiet sunshine. Only remained the hoof-marks in the meadow and the torn hillside to mark the boisterous trail of the life that had broken the peace of the place and passed on.

*Editor's note: Talented filmmakers the Coen brothers (*No Country for Old Men *and many others) have actually made a short movie of* "All Gold Canyon." *It is one of the vignettes in the film* The Ballad of Buster Scruggs. *As you would expect from Joel and Ethan Coen, the film is superbly photographed in a high-country setting and presented with care and accuracy, which would have made Jack London very proud, had he lived to see it.*

2

THE LURE OF BURIED TREASURE

BY RALPH D. PAINE

Buried treasure in America and the surrounding Caribbean islands once frequented by pirates are popular settings for literary journeys. Such treasures have existed in worldwide destinations, as writer Ralph D. Paine suggests in this wide review of treasure mania, a clarion call both irresistible and dangerous.

The language has no more boldly romantic words than *pirate* and *galleon* and the dullest imagination is apt to be kindled by any plausible dream of finding their lost treasures hidden on lonely beach or tropic key, or sunk fathoms deep in salt water. In the preface of that rare and exceedingly diverting volume, "The Pirates' Own Book," the unnamed author sums up the matter with so much gusto and with so gorgeously appetizing a flavor that he is worth quoting to this extent:

With the name of pirate is also associated ideas of rich plunder, caskets of buried jewels, chests of gold ingots, bags of outlandish coins, secreted in lonely, out of the way places, or buried about the wild shores of rivers and unexplored sea coasts, near rocks and trees bearing mysterious marks indicating where the treasure was hid. And as it is his invariable practice to secrete and bury his booty, and from the perilous life he leads, being often killed or captured, he can never revisit the spot again, therefore immense sums remain buried in those places and are irrevocably lost. Search is often made by persons who labor in anticipation of throwing up with their spade and pickaxe, gold bars, diamond crosses sparkling amongst the dirt, bags of golden doubloons and chests wedged close with moidores, ducats and pearls; but although great treasures lie hid in this way, it seldom happens that any is recovered.

In this tamed, prosaic age of ours, treasure-seeking might seem to be the peculiar province of fiction, but the fact is that expeditions are fitting out every little while, and mysterious schooners flitting from many ports, lured by grimy, tattered charts presumed to show where the hoards were hidden, or steering their courses by nothing more tangible than legend and surmise. As the Kidd tradition survives along the Atlantic coast, so on divers shores of other seas persist the same kind of wild tales, the more convincing of which are strikingly alike in that the lone survivor of the red-handed crew, having some-how escaped the hanging, shooting, or drowning that he handsomely merited, preserved a chart showing where the treasure had been hid. Unable to return to the place, he gave the parchment to some friend or shipmate, this dramatic transfer usually happening as a death-bed ceremony. The recipient, after digging in vain and heartily damning the departed pirate for his misleading landmarks and bearings, handed the chart down to the next generation.

It will be readily perceived that this is the stock motive of almost all buried treasure fiction, the trademark of a certain brand of adventure story, but it is really more entertaining to know that such charts and records exist and are made use of by the expeditions of the present day. Opportunity knocks at the door. He who would gamble in shares of such a speculation may find sun-burned, tarry gentlemen, from Seattle to Singapore, and from Capetown to New Zealand, eager to whisper curious information of charts and sailing directions, and to make sail and away.

Some of them are still seeking booty lost on Cocos Island off the coast of Costa Rica where a dozen expeditions have futilely sweated and dug; others have cast anchor in harbors of Guam and the Carolines; while as you run from Aden to Vladivostock, sailormen are never done with spinning yarns of treasure buried by the pirates of the Indian Ocean and the China Sea. Out from Callao the treasure hunters fare to Clipperton Island, or the Gallapagos group where the buccaneers with Dampier and Davis used to careen their ships, and from Valparaiso many an expedition has found its way to Juan Fernandez and Magellan Straits. The topsails of these salty argonauts have been sighted in recent years off the Salvages to the southward of Madeira where two millions of Spanish gold were buried in chests, and pick and shovel have been busy on rocky Trinidad in the South Atlantic which conceals vast stores of plate and jewels left there by pirates who looted the galleons of Lima.

Near Cape Vidal, on the coast of Zululand, lies the wreck of the notorious sailing vessel *Dorothea*, in whose hold is treasure to the amount of two million dollars in gold bars concealed beneath a flooring of cement. It was believed for some time that the ill-fated *Dorothea* was fleeing with the fortune of Oom Paul Kruger on board when she was cast ashore. The evidence goes to show, however, that certain officials of the Transvaal Government, before the Boer War, issued permits to several lawless adventurers, allowing them to engage in buying stolen gold from the mines. This illicit traffic flourished largely, and so successful was this particular combination that a ship was bought, the *Ernestine*, and after being overhauled and renamed the *Dorothea*, she secretly shipped the treasure on board in Delagoa Bay.

It was only the other day that a party of restless young Americans sailed in the old racing yacht *Mayflower* bound out to seek the wreck of a treasure galleon on the coast of Jamaica. Their vessel was dismasted and abandoned at sea, and they had all the adventure they yearned for. One of them, Roger Derby of Boston, of a family famed for its deep-water mariners in the olden times, ingenuously confessed some time later, and here you have the spirit of the true treasure-seeker:

"I am afraid that there is no information accessible in documentary or printed form of the wreck that we investigated a year ago. Most of it is hearsay, and when we went down there on a second trip after losing the *Mayflower*, we found little to prove that a galleon had been lost, barring some old cannon, flint rock ballast, and square iron bolts. We found absolutely no gold."

The coast of Madagascar, once haunted by free-booters who plundered the rich East Indiamen, is still ransacked by treasure seekers, and American soldiers in the Philippines indefatigably excavate the landscape of Luzon in the hope of finding the hoard of Spanish gold buried by the Chinese mandarin Chan Lu Suey in the eighteenth century. Every island of the West Indies and port of the Spanish Main abounds in legends of the mighty sea rogues whose hard fate it was to be laid by the heels before they could squander the gold that had been won with cutlass, boarding pike and carronade.

The spirit of true adventure lives in the soul of the treasure hunter. The odds may be a thousand to one that he will unearth a solitary doubloon, yet he is lured to undertake the most prodigious exertions by the keen zest of the game itself. The English novelist, George R. Sims, once expressed this state of mind very exactly. "Respectable citizens, tired of the melancholy sameness of a drab existence, cannot take to crape masks, dark lanterns, silent matches, and rope ladders, but they can all be off to a pirate island and search for treasure and return laden or empty without a stain upon their characters. I know a fine old pirate who sings a good song and has treasure islands at his fingers' ends. I think I can get together a band of adventurers, middle-aged men of established reputation in whom the public would have confidence, who would be only too glad to enjoy a year's romance."

Robert Louis Stevenson who dearly loved a pirate and wrote the finest treasure story of them all around a proper chart of his own devising, took Henry James to task for confessing that although he had been a child he had never been on a quest for buried treasure. "Here is indeed a willful paradox," exclaimed the author of "Treasure Island," "for if he has never been on a quest for buried treasure, it can be demonstrated that he has never been a child. There never was a child (unless Master James), but has hunted gold, and been a pirate, and a military commander, and a bandit of the mountains; but has fought, and suffered shipwreck and prison, and imbrued its little hands in gore, and gallantly retrieved the lost battle, and triumphantly protected innocence and beauty."

Mark Twain also indicated the singular isolation of Henry James by expressing precisely the same opinion in his immortal chronicle of the adventures of Tom Sawyer. "There comes a time in every rightly constructed boy's life when he has a raging desire to go somewhere and dig for buried treasure." And what an entrancing career Tom had planned for himself in an earlier chapter! "At the zenith of his fame, how he would suddenly appear at the old village and stalk into church, brown and weather-beaten, in his black velvet doublet and trunks, his great jack-boots, his crimson sash, his belt bristling with horse-pistols, his crime-rusted cutlass at his side, his slouch hat with waving plumes, his black flag unfurled, with the skull and cross-bones on it, and hear with swelling ecstasy the whisperings, 'It's Tom Sawyer the Pirate!—The Black Avenger of the Spanish Main.'"

When Tom and Huck Finn went treasure seeking they observed the time-honored rules of the game, as the following dialogue will recall to mind:

"Where'll we dig?" said Huck.

"Oh, most anywhere."

"Why, is it hid all around?"

"No, indeed it ain't. It's hid in mighty particular places, Huck, sometimes on islands, sometimes in rotten chests under the limb of an old dead tree, just where the shadow falls at midnight; but mostly under the floor in ha'nted houses."

"Who hides it?"

"Why, robbers, of course. Who'd you reckon, Sunday-school superintendents?"

"I don't know. If 'twas mine I wouldn't hide it; I'd spend it and have a good time."

"So would I. But robbers don't do that way. They always hide it and leave it there."

"Don't they come after it any more!"

"No, they think they will, but they generally forget the marks or else they die. Anyway, it lays there a long time and gets rusty; and by and by somebody finds an old yellow paper that tells how to find the marks,—a paper that's got to be ciphered over about a week because it's mostly signs and hy'roglyphics."

Hunting lost treasure is not work but a fascinating kind of play that belongs to the world of make believe. It appeals to that strain of boyishness which survives in the average man even though his pow be frosted, his reputation starched and conservative. It is, after all, an inherited taste handed down from the golden age of fairies. The folk-lore of almost every race is rich in buried treasure stories. The pirate with his stout sea chest hidden above high-water mark is lineally descended from the enchanting characters who lived in the shadow land of myth and fable. The hoard of Captain Kidd, although he was turned off at Execution Dock only two hundred years ago, has become as legendary as the dream of the pot of gold at the end of the rainbow.

Many a hard-headed farmer and fisherman of the New England coast believes that it is rash business to go digging for Kidd's treasure unless one carefully performs certain incantations designed to placate the ghostly guardian who aforetime sailed with Kidd and was slain by him after the hole was dug lest the secret might thus be revealed. And it is of course well known that if a word is spoken after the pick has clinked against the iron-bound chest or metal pot, the devil flies away with the treasure, leaving behind him only panic and a strong smell of brimstone.

Such curious superstitions as these, strongly surviving wherever pirate gold is sought, have been the common property of buried-treasure stories in all ages. The country-folk of Japan will tell you that if a pot of money is found a rice cake must be left in place of every coin taken away, and imitation money burned as an offering to any spirit that may be offended by the removal of the hoard. The natives of the West Indies explain that the buried wealth of the buccaneers is seldom found because the spirits that watch over it have a habit of whisking the treasure away to parts unknown as soon as ever the hiding-place is disturbed. Among the Bedouins is current the legend that immense treasures were concealed by Solomon beneath the foundations of Palmyra and that sapient monarch took the precaution of enlisting an army of jinns to guard the gold forever more.

In parts of Bohemia the peasants are convinced that a blue light hovers above the location of buried treasure, invisible to all mortal eyes save those of the person destined to find it. In many corners of the world there has long existed the belief in the occult efficacy of a black cock or a black cat in the equipment of a treasure quest which is also influenced by the particular phases of the moon. A letter written from Bombay as long ago as 1707, contained a quaint account of an incident inspired by this particular superstition.

Upon a dream of a Negro girl of Mahim that there was a Mine of Treasure, who being overheard relating it, Domo, Alvares, and some others went to the place and sacrificed a Cock and dugg the ground but found nothing. They go to Bundarra at Salsett, where disagreeing, the Government there takes notice of the same, and one of them, an inhabitant of Bombay, is sent to the Inquisition at Goa, which proceedings will discourage the Inhabitants. Wherefore the General is desired to issue a proclamation to release him, and if not restored in twenty days, no Roman Catholick Worship to be allowed on the Island.

A more recent chronicler, writing in *The Ceylon Times*, had this to say:

It is the belief of all Orientals that hidden treasures are under the guardianship of supernatural beings. The Cingalese divide the charge between the demons and the cobra da capello (guardian of the king's ankus in Kipling's story). Various charms are resorted to by those who wish to gain the treasure because the demons require a sacrifice. The blood of a human being is the most important, but so far as is known, the Cappowas have hitherto confined themselves to the sacrifice of a white cock, combining its blood with their own drawn from the hand or foot.

No more fantastic than this are the legends of which the British Isles yield a plentiful harvest. Thomas of Walsingham tells the tale of a Saracen physician who betook himself to Earl Warren of the fourteenth century to ask courteous permission that he might slay a dragon, or "loathly worm" which had its den at Bromfield near Ludlow and had wrought sad ravages on the Earl's lands. The Saracen overcame the monster, whether by means of his medicine chest or his trusty steel the narrator sayeth not, and then it was learned that a great hoard of gold was hidden in its foul den. Some men of Herefordshire sallied forth by night to search for the treasure, and were about to lay hands on it when retainers of the Earl of Warwick captured them and took the booty to their lord.

Blenkinsopp Castle is haunted by a very sorrowful White Lady. Her husband, Bryan de Blenkinsopp, was uncommonly greedy of gold, which he loved better than his wife, and she, being very jealous and angry, was mad enough to hide from him a chest of treasure so heavy that twelve strong men were needed to lift it. Later she was overtaken by remorse because of this undutiful behavior and to this day her uneasy ghost flits about the castle, supposedly seeking the spirit of Bryan de Blenkinsopp in order that she may tell him what she did with his pelf.

When Corfe Castle in Dorsetshire was besieged by Cromwell's troops, Lady Bankes conducted a heroic defense. Betrayed by one of her own garrison, and despairing of holding out longer, she threw all the plate and jewels into a very deep well in the castle yard, and pronounced a curse against anyone who should try to find it ere she returned. She then ordered the traitor to be hanged, and surrendered the place. The treasure was never found, and perhaps later owners have been afraid of the militant ghost of Lady Bankes.

From time immemorial, tradition had it that a great treasure was buried near the Kibble in Lancashire. A saying had been handed down that anyone standing on the hill at Walton-le-Dale and looking up the valley toward the site of ancient Richester would gaze over the greatest treasure that England had ever known. Digging was undertaken at intervals during several centuries, until in 1841 laborers accidentally excavated a mass of silver ornaments, armlets, neck-chains, amulets and rings, weighing together about a thousand ounces, and more than seven thousand silver coins, mostly of King Alfred's time, all enclosed in a leaden case only three feet beneath the surface of the ground. Many of these ornaments and coins are to be seen at the British Museum.

On a farm in the Scotch parish of Lesmahagow is a boulder beneath which is what local tradition calls "a kettle full, a boat full, and a bull's hide full of gold that is Katie Nevin's hoord." And for ages past 'tis well known that a pot of gold has lain at the bottom of a pool at the tail of a water-fall under Crawfurdland Bridge, three miles from Kilmarnock. The last attempt to fish it up was made by one of the lairds of the place who diverted the stream and emptied the pool, and the implements of the workmen actually rang against the precious kettle when a mysterious voice was heard to cry:

"Paw! Paw! Crawfurdland's tower's in a law."

The laird and his servants scampered home to find out whether the tower had been "laid law," but the alarm was only a stratagem of the spirit that did sentry duty over the treasure. When the party returned to the pool, it was filled to the brim and the water was "running o'er the linn," which was an uncanny thing to see, and the laird would have nothing more to do with treasure seeking.

The people of Glenary in the Highlands long swore by the legend that golden treasure was hidden in their valley and that it would not be found until sought for by the son of a stranger. At length, while a newly drained field was being plowed, a large rock was shattered by blasting, and under it were found many solid gold bracelets of antique pattern and cunningly ornamented. The old people knew that the prophecy had come true, for the youth who held the plow was the son of an Englishman, a rare being in those parts a few generations ago.

Everyone knows that Ireland is fairly peppered with "crocks o' goold" which the peasantry would have dug up long before this, but the treasure is invariably in the keeping of "the little black men" and they raise the divil and all with the bold intruder, and lucky he is if he is not snatched away, body, soul, and breeches. Many a fine lad has left home just before midnight with a mattock under his arm, and maybe there was a terrible clap of thunder and that was the last of him except the empty hole and the mattock beside it which his friends found next morning.

In France treasure seeking has been at times a popular madness. The traditions of the country are singularly alluring, and perhaps the most romantic of them is that of the "Great Treasure of Gourdon" which is said to have existed since the reign of Clovis in the sixth century. The chronicle of all the wealth buried in the cemetery of this convent at Gourdon in the Department of the Lot has been preserved, including detailed lists of gold and silver, rubies, emeralds and pearls. The convent was sacked and plundered by the Normans, and the treasurer, or custodian, who had buried all the valuables of the religious houses under the sway of the same abbot, was murdered while trying to escape to the feudal seignor of Gourdon with the crosier of the lord abbot. "The head of the crosier was of solid gold," says an ancient manuscript, "and the rubies with which it was studded of such wondrous size that at one single blow the soldier who tore it from the monk's grasp and used it as a weapon against him, beat in his brains as with a sledge-hammer."

Not only through the Middle Ages was the search resumed from time to time, but from the latter days of the reign of Louis XIV until the Revolution, tradition relates that the cemetery of the convent was ransacked at frequent intervals. At length, in 1842, the quest was abandoned after antiquarians, geologists, and engineers had gravely agreed that further excavation would be futile. The French treasure seekers went elsewhere and then a peasant girl confused the savants by discovering what was undeniably a part of the lost riches of Gourdon. She was driving home the cows from a pasture of the abbey lands when a shower caused her to take shelter in a hollow scooped out of a sandbank by laborers mending the road. Some of the earth caved in upon her and while she was freeing herself, down rolled a salver, a paten, and a flagon, all of pure gold, richly chased and studded with emeralds and rubies. These articles were taken to Paris and advertised for sale by auction, the Government bidding them in and placing them in the museum of the Bibliotheque.

During the reign of Napoleon III there died a very famous treasure seeker, one Ducasse, who believed that he was about to discover "the master treasure" (*le maitre tresor*) said to be among the ruins of the ancient Belgian Abbey of Orval. Ducasse was a builder by trade and had gained a large fortune in government contracts every sou of which he wasted in exploring at Orval. It was alleged that the treasure had been buried by the monks and that the word NEMO carved on the tomb of the last abbott held the key to the location of the hiding-place.

In Mexico one hears similar tales of vast riches buried by religious orders when menaced by war or expulsion. One of these is to be found in the south-western part of the state of Chihuahua where a great gorge is cut by the Rio Verde. In this remote valley are the ruins of a church built by the Jesuits, and when they were about to be driven from their settlement they sealed up and destroyed all traces of a fabulously rich mine in which was buried millions of bullion. Instead of the more or less stereotyped ghosts familiar as sentinels over buried treasure, these lost hoards of Mexico are haunted by a specter even more disquieting than phantom pirates or "little black men." It is "The Weeping Woman" who makes strong men cross themselves and shiver in their serapes, and many have heard or seen her. A member of a party seeking buried treasure in the heart of the Sierra Madre mountains solemnly affirmed as follows:

We were to measure, at night, a certain distance from a cliff which was to be found by the relative positions of three tall trees. It was on a bleak tableland nine thousand feet above the sea. The wind chilled us to the marrow, although we were only a little to the north of the Tropic of Cancer. We rode all night and waited for the dawn in the darkest and coldest hours of those altitudes. By the light of pitch pine torches we consulted a map and decided that we had found the right place. We rode forward a little and brushed against three soft warm things. Turning in our saddles, by the flare of our torches held high above our heads we beheld three corpses swaying in the wind. A wailing cry of a woman's voice came from close at hand, and we fled as if pursued by a thousand demons. My comrades assured me that the Weeping Woman had brushed past us in her eternal flight.

This is a singular narrative but it would not be playing fair to doubt it. To be over-critical of buried treasure stories is to clip the wings of romance and to condemn the spirit of adventure to a pedestrian gait. All these tales are true, or men of sane and sober repute would not go a-treasure hunting by land and sea, and so long as they have a high-hearted, boyish faith in their mysterious charts and hazy information, doubters make a poor show of themselves and stand confessed as thin-blooded dullards who never were young. Scattered legends of many climes have been mentioned at random to show that treasure is everywhere enveloped in a glamour peculiarly its own. The base iconoclast may perhaps demolish Santa Claus (which God forbid), but industrious dreamers will be digging for the gold of Captain Kidd, long after the last Christmas stocking shall have been pinned above the fireplace.

There are no conscious liars among the tellers of treasure tales. The spell is upon them. They believe their own yarns, and they prove their faith by their back-breaking works with pick and shovel. Here, for example, is a specimen, chosen at hazard, one from a thousand cut from the same cloth. This is no modern Ananias speaking but a gray-bearded, God-fearing clam-digger of Jewell's Island in Casco Bay on the coast of Maine.

I can't remember when the treasure hunters first began coming to this island, but as long ago as my father's earliest memories they used to dig for gold up and down the shore. That was in the days when they were superstitious enough to spill lamb's blood along the ground where they dug in order to keep away the devil and his imps. I can remember fifty years ago when they brought a girl down here and mesmerized her to see if she could not lead them to the hidden wealth.

The biggest mystery, though, of all the queer things that have happened here in the last hundred years was the arrival of the man from St. John's when I was a youngster. He claimed to have the very chart showing the exact spot where Kidd's gold was buried. He said he had got it from an old negro in St. John's who was with Captain Kidd when he was coasting the islands in this bay. He showed up here when old Captain Chase that lived here then was off to sea in his vessel. So he waited around a few days till the captain returned, for he wanted to use a mariner's compass to locate the spot according to the directions on the chart.

When Captain Chase came ashore the two went off up the beach together, and the man from St. John's was never seen again, neither hide nor hair of him, and it is plumb certain that he wasn't set off in a boat from Jewell's.

The folks here found a great hole dug on the southeast shore which looked as if a large chest had been lifted out of it. Of course conclusions were drawn, but nobody got at the truth. Four years ago someone found a skeleton in the woods, unburied, simply dropped into a crevice in the rocks with a few stones thrown over it. No one knows whose body it was, although some say,—but never mind about that. This old Captain Jonathan Chase was said to have been a pirate, and his house was full of underground passages and sliding panels and queer contraptions, such as no honest, law-abiding man could have any use for.

The worthy Benjamin Franklin was an admirable guide for young men, a sound philosopher, and a sagacious statesman, but he cannot be credited with romantic imagination. He would have been the last person in the world to lead a buried treasure expedition or to find pleasure in the company of the most eminent and secretive pirate that ever scuttled a ship or made mysterious marks upon a well-thumbed chart plentifully spattered with candle-grease and rum. He even took pains to discourage the diverting industry of treasure seeking as it flourished among his Quaker neighbors and discharged this formidable broadside in the course of a series of essays known as "The Busy-Body Series":

There are among us great numbers of honest artificers and laboring people, who, fed with a vain hope of suddenly growing rich, neglect their business, almost to the ruining of themselves and families, and voluntarily endure abundance of fatigue in a fruitless search after imaginary hidden treasure. They wander through the woods and bushes by day to discover the marks and signs; at midnight they repair to the hopeful spots with spades and pickaxes; full of expectation, they labor violently, trembling at the same time in every joint through fear of certain malicious demons, who are said to haunt and guard such places.

At length a mighty hole is dug, and perhaps several cart-loads of earth thrown out; but, alas, no keg or iron pot is found. No seaman's chest crammed with Spanish pistoles, or weighty pieces of eight! They conclude that, through some mistake in the procedure, some rash word spoken, or some rule of art neglected, the guardian spirit had power to sink it deeper into the earth, and convey it out of their reach. Yet, when a man is once infatuated, he is so far from being discouraged by ill success that he is rather animated to double his industry, and will try again and again in a hundred different places in hopes of meeting at last with some lucky hit, that shall at once sufficiently reward him for all his expenses of time and labor.

This odd humor of digging for money, through a belief that much has been hidden by pirates formerly frequenting the (Schuylkill) river, has for several years been mighty prevalent among us; insomuch that you can hardly walk half a mile out of the town on any side without observing several pits dug with that design, and perhaps some lately opened. Men otherwise of very good sense have been drawn into this practice through an overweening desire of sudden wealth, and an easy credulity of what they so earnestly wished might be true. There seems to be some peculiar charm in the conceit of finding money and if the sands of Schuylkill were so much mixed with small grains of gold that a man might in a day's time with care and application get together to the value of half a crown, I make no question but we should find several people employed there that can with ease earn five shillings a day at their proper trade.

Many are the idle stories told of the private success of some people, by which others are encouraged to proceed; and the astrologers, with whom the country swarms at this time, are either in the belief of these things themselves, or find their advantage in persuading others to believe them; for they are often consulted about the critical times for digging, the methods of laying the spirit, and the like whimseys, which renders them very necessary to, and very much caressed by these poor, deluded money hunters.

There is certainly something very bewitching in the pursuit after mines of gold and silver and other valuable metals, and many have been ruined by it . . .

Let honest Peter Buckram, who has long without success been a searcher after hidden money, reflect on this, and be reclaimed from that unaccountable folly. Let him consider that every stitch he takes when he is on his shopboard, is picking up part of a grain of gold that will in a few days' time amount to a pistole; and let Faber think the same of every nail he drives, or every stroke with his plane. Such thoughts may make them industrious, and, in consequence, in time they may be wealthy.

But how absurd it is to neglect a certain profit for such a ridiculous whimsey; to spend whole days at the "George" in company with an idle pretender to astrology, contriving schemes to discover what was never hidden, and forgetful how carelessly business is managed at home in their absence; to leave their wives and a warm bed at midnight (no matter if it rain, hail, snow, or blow a hurricane, provided that be the critical hour), and fatigue themselves with the violent digging for what they shall never find, and perhaps getting a cold that may cost their lives, or at least disordering themselves so as to be fit for no business beside for some days after. Surely this is nothing less than the most egregious folly and madness.

I shall conclude with the words of the discreet friend Agricola of Chester County when he gave his son a good plantation. "My son," said he, "I give thee now a valuable parcel of land; I assure thee I have found a considerable quantity of gold by digging there; thee mayest do the same; but thee must carefully observe this, *Never to dig more than plough-deep.*"

For once the illustrious Franklin shot wide of the mark. These treasure hunters of Philadelphia, who had seen with their own eyes more than one notorious pirate, even Blackbeard himself, swagger along Front Street or come roaring out of the Blue Anchor Tavern by Dock Creek, were finding their reward in the coin of romance. Digging mighty holes for a taskmaster would have been irksome, stupid business indeed, even for five shillings a day. They got a fearsome kind of enjoyment in "trembling violently through fear of certain malicious demons." And honest Peter Buckram no doubt discovered that life was more zestful when he was plying shovel and pickaxe, or whispering with an astrologer in a corner of the "George" than during the flat hours of toil with shears and goose. If the world had charted its course by Poor Richard's Almanac, there would be a vast deal more thrift and sober industry than exists, but no room for the spirit of adventure which reckons not its returns in dollars and cents.

There are many kinds of lost treasure, by sea and by land. Some of them, however, lacking the color of romance and the proper backgrounds of motive and incident, have no stories worth telling. For instance, there were almost five thousand wrecks on the Great Lakes during a period of twenty years, and these lost vessels carried down millions of treasure or property worth trying to recover. One steamer had five hundred thousand dollars' worth of copper in her hold. Divers and submarine craft and wrecking companies have made many attempts to recover these vanished riches, and with considerable success, now and then fishing up large amounts of gold coin and bullion. It goes without saying that the average sixteen-year-old boy could extract not one solitary thrill from a tale of lost treasure in the Great Lakes, even though the value might be fairly fabulous. But let him hear that a number of Spanish coins have been washed up by the waves on a beach of Yucatan and the discovery has set the natives to searching for the buried treasure of Jean Lafitte, the "Pirate of the Gulf," and our youngster pricks up his ears.

Many noble merchantmen in modern times have foundered or crashed ashore in various seas with large fortunes in their treasure rooms, and these are sought by expeditions, but because these ships were not galleons nor carried a freightage of doubloons and pieces of eight, most of them must be listed in the catalogue of undistinguished sea tragedies. The distinction is really obvious. The treasure story must have the picaresque flavor or at least concern itself with bold deeds done by strong men in days gone by. Like wine its bouquet is improved by age.

It is the fashion to consider lost treasure as the peculiar property of pirates and galleons, and yet what has become of the incredibly vast riches of all the vanished kings, despots, and soldiers who plundered the races of men from the beginnings of history? Where is the loot of ancient Home that was buried with Alaric! Where is the dazzling treasure of Samarcand? Where is the wealth of Antioch, and where the jewels which Solomon gave the Queen of Sheba? During thousands of years of warfare the treasures of the Old World could be saved from the conqueror only by hiding them underground, and in countless instances the sword must have slain those who knew the secret. When Genghis Khan swept across Russia with his hordes of savage Mongols towns and cities were blotted out as by fire, and doubtless those of the slaughtered population who had gold and precious stones buried them and there they still await the treasure seeker. What was happening everywhere during the ruthless ages of conquest is indicated by this bit of narrative told by a native banker of India to W. Forbes Mitchell, author of "Reminiscences of the Great Mutiny":

You know how anxious the late Maharajah Scindia was to get back the fortress of Gwalior, but very few knew the real cause prompting him. That was a concealed horde of sixty *crores* (sixty millions sterling) of rupees in certain vaults within the fortress, over which British sentinels had been walking for thirty years, never suspecting the wealth hidden under their feet. Long before the British Government restored the fortress to the Maharajah everyone who knew the entrance to the vaults was dead except one man and he was extremely old. Although he was in good health he might have died any day. If this had happened, the treasure might have been lost to the owner forever and to the world for ages, because there was only one method of entrance and it was most cunningly concealed. On all sides, except for this series of blind passages, the vaults were surrounded by solid rock.

The Maharajah was in such a situation that he must either get back his fortress or divulge the secret of the existence of the treasure to the British Government, and risk losing it by confiscation. As soon as possession of the fortress was restored to him, and even before the British troops had left Gwalior territory, masons were brought from Benares, after being sworn to secrecy in the Temple of the Holy Cow. They were blindfolded and driven to the place where they were to labor. There they were kept as prisoners until the hidden treasure had been examined and verified when the hole was again sealed up and the workmen were once more blindfolded and taken back to Benares in the custody of an armed escort.

3

THE SPELL OF THE YUKON

BY ROBERT W. SERVICE

In verse as powerful as any prose ever written, the now-legendary author Robert Service (1874–1958) gives the Yukon Gold Rush a felt life, ranging from the pain of hardships to the ultimate truths of dreams ended.

I wanted the gold, and I sought it,
I scrabbled and mucked like a slave.
Was it famine or scurvy—I fought it;
I hurled my youth into a grave.
I wanted the gold, and I got it—
Came out with a fortune last fall,—
Yet somehow life's not what I thought it,
And somehow the gold isn't all.

No! There's the land. (Have you seen it?)
It's the cussedest land that I know,
From the big, dizzy mountains that screen it
To the deep, deathlike valleys below.
Some say God was tired when He made it;
Some say it's a fine land to shun;
Maybe; but there's some as would trade it
For no land on earth—and I'm one.

You come to get rich (damned good reason);
You feel like an exile at first;
You hate it like hell for a season,
And then you are worse than the worst.
It grips you like some kinds of sinning;

It twists you from foe to a friend;
It seems it's been since the beginning;
It seems it will be to the end.

I've stood in some mighty-mouthed hollow
That's plumb-full of hush to the brim;
I've watched the big, husky sun wallow
In crimson and gold, and grow dim,
Till the moon set the pearly peaks gleaming,
And the stars tumbled out, neck and crop;
And I've thought that I surely was dreaming,
With the peace o' the world piled on top.

The summer—no sweeter was ever;
The sunshiny woods all athrill;
The grayling aleap in the river,
The bighorn asleep on the hill.
The strong life that never knows harness;
The wilds where the caribou call;
The freshness, the freedom, the farness—
O God! how I'm stuck on it all.

The winter! the brightness that blinds you,
The white land locked tight as a drum,
The cold fear that follows and finds you,
The silence that bludgeons you dumb.
The snows that are older than history,
The woods where the weird shadows slant;
The stillness, the moonlight, the mystery,
I've bade 'em good-by—but I can't.

There's a land where the mountains are nameless,
And the rivers all run God knows where;
There are lives that are erring and aimless,
And deaths that just hang by a hair;
There are hardships that nobody reckons;
There are valleys unpeopled and still;
There's a land—oh, it beckons and beckons,
And I want to go back—and I will.

They're making my money diminish;
I'm sick of the taste of champagne.
Thank God! when I'm skinned to a finish
I'll pike to the Yukon again.
I'll fight—and you bet it's no sham-fight;
It's hell!—but I've been there before;
And it's better than this by a damsite—
So me for the Yukon once more.

There's gold, and it's haunting and haunting;
It's luring me on as of old;
Yet it isn't the gold that I'm wanting
So much as just finding the gold.
It's the great, big, broad land 'way up yonder,
It's the forests where silence has lease;
It's the beauty that thrills me with wonder,
It's the stillness that fills me with peace.

4

GOLD AND GRIZZLIES

BY FRONA EUNICE WAIT

Before the goldfields of the far north lured prospectors, California was the place to seek treasure. The riches the gold-seekers found there were guarded by great beasts, the likes of which had never been seen.

If any of the boys and girls born in the United States were asked "Where is the land of gold?" they would answer "It is California," and if any of the children born in California were asked "What is El Dorado?" they would say "Why, that means the land of gold."

So it does and for two reasons.

Cortez named it California after the heroine of a romance of chivalry he had read when he was in Spain. The book said there was an island on the right hand of the Indies very near the terrestrial Paradise, peopled with black women, who were Amazons, and wore gold ornaments in great profusion. Down in his heart Cortez cherished the hope that he might find the northwest passage to India, not because he cared very much for science, but because he believed the most extravagant stories about the silks, spices, sweet-smelling gums and rare gems to be found there. His ill-gotten Mexican gold did him very little good, and was soon all expended, and he was anxious to find some other country to conquer. The very next year after the death of Montezuma, Cortez heard of the Land of Gold, and came over to a cove on the Pacific Coast of Mexico where he laid out a town and built some ships for the purpose of finding the new wonderland. All he ever discovered was the peninsula of Lower California, where the Indians already knew about the pearl fisheries. This was what he thought was an island, and what he named California.

One of his officers sailed around the island of St. Thomas, and on a Sunday morning he said he saw a merman swimming close to his ship.

"It came alongside the vessel," he declared, "and raised its head and looked at us two or three times. It was as full of antics as a monkey. Sometimes it would dive, and then raise up out of the water and wash its face with its hands. Finally a sea bird drove it away."

Of course he was mistaken, for what he really did see was either a walrus or a big seal as both animals abound in the Pacific Ocean.

It was more than three hundred years after Cabrillo sailed into the Gate of Palms at the entrance to the bay of San Diego, before gold was discovered in California. The country had been settled by Spanish Cavaliers and padres and there were missions for the teaching of the Indians. Mexico had rebelled against the King of Spain and the United States had made war on Mexico and won. Then a man by the name of Marshall found some free gold. It was in the sand at the bottom of a ditch he was digging to get water to run a sawmill he was building. He knew at once that the bright yellow pebbles he held in his hands were gold, so he hurried to the men at work on the watershed and said: "I have found it!" and that is what the motto—Eureka!—on the state shield of California really means.

"What is it you have found, Mr. Marshall?" asked the men.

"Gold!" he exclaimed, excitedly. The men threw down their tools and gathered about him to examine the new find.

"No, no; you are mistaken," they said, when they had turned the pebbles over, and held them to the light, and hammered them with a stone.

"I am certain that it is," he stoutly maintained, but they only laughed at him. He paid no attention to them but turned on the water the next night. Then he picked up all the yellow lumps he found in the sand, and putting them into a little bag hastened to the man for whom he was building the mill, and said: "I have found gold at the sawmill, and want you to come and see for yourself."

His employer tested and weighed the shining mass carefully, and finally said: "You are right. It is real gold. Go back to the mill, but say nothing until we get it finished. If you do the men will quit work and we shall have no one to take their places."

~~~~~~

But the secret was too good to keep, and in a few days the whole country raised the same sordid cry of "gold, gold, gold," which had brought the Spaniards to the coast. In less than a year eighty thousand people came to California looking for gold. From an independent republic, California became a state and with its admission into the Union the search for El Dorado passed from Spanish into American hands. Both the padres and Cavaliers in California as elsewhere in the Americas enslaved the Indians in a system of peonage which thinned out their ranks, and led to many hostile outbreaks before they were finally subdued. The gold seekers had to do some of the fighting, but they did not rob and pillage the country, nor were they allowed to be unnecessarily cruel. One of our great writers has said of the Indian: "The red man of America has something peculiarly sensitive in his nature. He shrinks instinctively from the rude touch of a foreign hand. Like some of the dumb creatures he pines and dies in captivity. If today we see them with their energies broken we simply learn from that what a terrible thing is slavery. In their faltering steps and meek and melancholy aspect we read the sad characteristics of a conquered race."

His faith in the traditions of his forefathers, the belief that the Golden Hearted would come again to bring him all that his heart desired finally enslaved and ruined him.

If we pity the Indian we must also feel sorry for the miserable ending of all the Spanish leaders who searched for El Dorado. Columbus spent the last years of his life in prison; Balboa, who discovered the Pacific

Ocean, was treacherously executed and lies in an unknown grave near Panama; Pizarro was assassinated and buried in Peru; Magellan was killed by the natives in the Philippine Islands; Cortez was accused of strangling his wife to death, and finally deprived of all honors and wealth; Guzman died in poverty and distress while Coronado was said to be insane after his return to Mexico. For the crime and violence done by Spain in these expeditions she has not only lost all the revenues, but no longer owns a foot of land in any part of the new world.

Let us be thankful that the wisdom and liberty of our own government has saved us from making such terrible mistakes, and doing such grievous wrongs in our attempts to find El Dorado. The brave men and women who crossed the plains long before we had a railroad were willing to work for the riches they wanted. They did not come with the idea of robbing anybody, and when they found the gold they were generous and kind to less fortunate neighbors and friends.

"In this land of sunshine and flowers," they said, "we find gold in the crops of the chickens we have for our Sunday dinners, and our children build doll-houses with the odd-shaped nuggets given to them by the big-hearted miners."

It is hard to imagine the stirring times that followed. Everybody had the gold fever, and in crossing the plains they heard the name El Dorado as soon as they came near where Coronado had been. Some of them made up a song about it, which was for many years very popular among the men in the mining camps. This is one verse of it:

We'll rock the cradle around Pike's Peak
In search of the gold dust that we seek,
The Indians ask us why we're here
We tell them we're born as free as the air,
And oh!

Boys ho!
To the mountains we will go
For there is plenty of gold
Out West we are told
In the new El Dorado.

Many of the emigrants sickened and died on the way; others were killed by the hostile Indians, and all were subjected to a life of hardship and toil, because they were the builders of a new commonwealth. Once in California they found many trying situations, not the least of which was an occasional fight with the huge grizzly bears that roamed through the forests. Many times the men were obliged to organize a hunt for the purpose of ridding a district of a nest of grizzlies. Not only would the bears fight ferociously, but they did not hesitate to go into a corral and carry off calves, hogs and sheep under the very eyes of the owner.

"Never for a moment imagine that a grizzly bear will run from you," said the leader of a hunting party filling his powder horn and putting a box of caps into his pocket. "Take good aim at the center of his forehead. Otherwise one shot will not kill him, and remember that he cannot climb. If you get into close quarters, try to get up a tree as fast as you can."

5
~

YOUNG TREASURE HUNTERS

Huck Finn and Tom Sawyer

BY MARK TWAIN

The argument that Mark Twain was America's greatest writer can be made with force. He was not only prolific, but his prose reeks of freshness and vividness, unlike many of the stodgy writers of his day (1835–1910). In his book Tom Sawyer, *his leading character teams up with the protagonist of an earlier book,* Huckleberry Finn. *Here Tom and Huck set out on a treasure-seeking jaunt that turns into a real adventure. (Editor's note: this story has been edited from the original.)*

There comes a time in every rightly-constructed boy's life when he has a raging desire to go somewhere and dig for hidden treasure. This desire suddenly came upon Tom one day. He sallied out to find Joe Harper, but failed of success. Next he sought Ben Rogers; he had gone fishing. Presently he stumbled upon Huck Finn the Red-Handed. Huck would answer. Tom took him to a private place and opened the matter to him confidentially. Huck was willing. Huck was always willing to take a hand in any enterprise that offered entertainment and required no capital, for he had a troublesome superabundance of that sort of time which is not money. "Where'll we dig?" said Huck.

"Oh, most anywhere."

"Why, is it hid all around?"

"No, indeed it ain't. It's hid in mighty particular places, Huck— sometimes on islands, sometimes in rotten chests under the end of a limb of an old dead tree, just where the shadow falls at midnight; but mostly under the floor in ha'nted houses."

"Who hides it?"

"Why, robbers, of course—who'd you reckon? Sunday-school sup'rintendents?"

"I don't know. If 'twas mine I wouldn't hide it; I'd spend it and have a good time."

"So would I. But robbers don't do that way. They always hide it and leave it there."

"Don't they come after it any more?"

"No, they think they will, but they generally forget the marks, or else they die. Anyway, it lays there a long time and gets rusty; and by and by somebody finds an old yellow paper that tells how to find the marks—a paper that's got to be ciphered over about a week because it's mostly signs and hy'roglyphics."

"Hyro—which?"

"Hy'roglyphics—pictures and things, you know, that don't seem to mean anything."

"Have you got one of them papers, Tom?"

"No."

"Well then, how you going to find the marks?"

"I don't want any marks. They always bury it under a ha'nted house or on an island, or under a dead tree that's got one limb sticking out. Well, we've tried Jackson's Island a little, and we can try it again some time; and there's the old ha'nted house up the Still-House branch, and there's lots of dead-limb trees—dead loads of 'em."

"Is it under all of them?"

"How you talk! No!"

"Then how you going to know which one to go for?"

"Go for all of 'em!"

"Why, Tom, it'll take all summer."

"Well, what of that? Suppose you find a brass pot with a hundred dollars in it, all rusty and gray, or rotten chest full of di'monds. How's that?"

Huck's eyes glowed.

"That's bully. Plenty bully enough for me. Just you gimme the hundred dollars and I don't want no di'monds."

"All right. But I bet you I ain't going to throw off on di'monds. Some of 'em's worth twenty dollars apiece—there ain't any, hardly, but's worth six bits or a dollar."

"No! Is that so?"

"Cert'nly—anybody'll tell you so. Hain't you ever seen one, Huck?"

"Not as I remember."

"Oh, kings have slathers of them."

"Well, I don' know no kings, Tom."

"I reckon you don't. But if you was to go to Europe you'd see a raft of 'em hopping around."

"Do they hop?"

"Hop?—your granny! No!"

"Well, what did you say they did, for?"

"Shucks, I only meant you'd *see* 'em—not hopping, of course—what do they want to hop for?—but I mean you'd just see 'em—scattered around, you know, in a kind of a general way. Like that old humpbacked Richard."

"Richard? What's his other name?"

"He didn't have any other name. Kings don't have any but a given name."

"No?"

"But they don't."

"Well, if they like it, Tom, all right; but I don't want to be a king and have only just a given name. . . . But say—where you going to dig first?"

"Well, I don't know. S'pose we tackle that old dead-limb tree on the hill t'other side of Still-House branch?"

"I'm agreed."

So they got a crippled pick and a shovel, and set out on their three-mile tramp. They arrived hot and panting, and threw themselves down in the shade of a neighboring elm to rest and have a smoke.

"I like this," said Tom.

"So do I."

"Say, Huck, if we find a treasure here, what you going to do with your share?"

"Well, I'll have pie and a glass of soda every day, and I'll go to every circus that comes along. I bet I'll have a gay time."

"Well, ain't you going to save any of it?"

"Save it? What for?"

"Why, so as to have something to live on, by and by."

"Oh, that ain't any use. Pap would come back to thish-yer town some day and get his claws on it if I didn't hurry up, and I tell you he'd clean it out pretty quick. What you going to do with yourn, Tom?"

"I'm going to buy a new drum, and a sure'nough sword, and a red necktie and a bull pup, and get married."

"Married!"

"That's it."

"Tom, you—why, you ain't in your right mind."

"Wait—you'll see."

"Well, that's the foolishest thing you could do. Look at pap and my mother. Fight! Why, they used to fight all the time. I remember, mighty well."

"That ain't anything. The girl I'm going to marry won't fight."

"Tom, I reckon they're all alike. They'll all comb a body. Now you better think 'bout this awhile. I tell you you better. What's the name of the gal?"

"It ain't a gal at all—it's a girl."

"It's all the same, I reckon; some says gal, some says girl—both's right, like enough. Anyway, what's her name, Tom?"

"I'll tell you some time—not now."

"All right—that'll do. Only if you get married I'll be more lonesomer than ever."

"No you won't. You'll come and live with me. Now stir out of this and we'll go to digging."

They worked and sweated for half an hour. No result. They toiled another half hour. Still no result. Huck said:

"Do they always bury it as deep as this?"

"Sometimes—not always. Not generally. I reckon we haven't got the right place."

So they chose a new spot and began again. The labor dragged a little, but still they made progress. They pegged away in silence for some time. Finally Huck leaned on his shovel, swabbed the beaded drops from his brow with his sleeve, and said:

"Where you going to dig next, after we get this one?"

"I reckon maybe we'll tackle the old tree that's over yonder on Cardiff Hill back of the widow's."

"I reckon that'll be a good one. But won't the widow take it away from us, Tom? It's on her land."

"*She* take it away! Maybe she'd like to try it once. Whoever finds one of these hid treasures, it belongs to him. It don't make any difference whose land it's on."

That was satisfactory. The work went on. By and by Huck said:

"Blame it, we must be in the wrong place again. What do you think?"

"It is mighty curious, Huck. I don't understand it. Sometimes witches interfere. I reckon maybe that's what's the trouble now."

"Shucks! Witches ain't got no power in the daytime."

"Well, that's so. I didn't think of that. Oh, I know what the matter is! What a blamed lot of fools we are! You got to find out where the shadow of the limb falls at midnight, and that's where you dig!"

"Then consound it, we've fooled away all this work for nothing. Now hang it all, we got to come back in the night. It's an awful long way. Can you get out?"

"I bet I will. We've got to do it tonight, too, because if somebody sees these holes they'll know in a minute what's here and they'll go for it."

"Well, I'll come around and maow tonight."

"All right. Let's hide the tools in the bushes."

The boys were there that night, about the appointed time. They sat in the shadow waiting. It was a lonely place, and an hour made solemn by old traditions. Spirits whispered in the rustling leaves, ghosts lurked in the murky nooks, the deep baying of a hound floated up out of the distance, an owl answered with his sepulchral note. The boys were subdued by these solemnities, and talked little. By and by they judged that twelve had come; they marked where the shadow fell, and began to dig. Their hopes commenced to rise. Their interest grew stronger, and their industry kept pace with it. The hole deepened and still deepened, but every time their hearts jumped to hear the pick strike upon something, they only suffered a new disappointment. It was only a stone or a chunk. At last Tom said:

"It ain't any use, Huck, we're wrong again."

"Well, but we *can't* be wrong. We spotted the shadder to a dot."

"I know it, but then there's another thing."

"What's that?"

"Why, we only guessed at the time. Like enough it was too late or too early."

Huck dropped his shovel.

"That's it," said he. "That's the very trouble. We got to give this one up. We can't ever tell the right time, and besides this kind of thing's too awful, here this time of night with witches and ghosts a-fluttering around so. I feel as if something's behind me all the time; and I'm afeard to turn around, becuz maybe there's others in front a-waiting for a chance. I been creeping all over, ever since I got here."

"Well, I've been pretty much so, too, Huck. They most always put in a dead man when they bury a treasure under a tree, to look out for it."

"Lordy!"

"Yes, they do. I've always heard that."

"Tom, I don't like to fool around much where there's dead people. A body's bound to get into trouble with 'em, sure."

"I don't like to stir 'em up, either. S'pose this one here was to stick his skull out and say something!"

"Don't Tom! It's awful."

"Well, it just is. Huck, I don't feel comfortable a bit."

"Say, Tom, let's give this place up, and try somewheres else."

"All right, I reckon we better."

"What'll it be?"

Tom considered awhile; and then said:

"The ha'nted house. That's it!"

"Blame it, I don't like ha'nted houses, Tom. Why, they're a dern sight worse'n dead people. Dead people might talk, maybe, but they don't come sliding around in a shroud, when you ain't noticing, and peep over your shoulder all of a sudden and grit their teeth, the way a ghost does. I couldn't stand such a thing as that, Tom—nobody could."

"Yes, but, Huck, ghosts don't travel around only at night. They won't hender us from digging there in the daytime."

"Well, that's so. But you know mighty well people don't go about that ha'nted house in the day nor the night."

"Well, that's mostly because they don't like to go where a man's been murdered, anyway—but nothing's ever been seen around that house except in the night—just some blue lights slipping by the windows—no regular ghosts."

"Well, where you see one of them blue lights flickering around, Tom, you can bet there's a ghost mighty close behind it. It stands to reason. Becuz you know that they don't anybody but ghosts use 'em."

"Yes, that's so. But anyway they don't come around in the daytime, so what's the use of our being afeard?"

"Well, all right. We'll tackle the ha'nted house if you say so—but I reckon it's taking chances."

They had started down the hill by this time. There in the middle of the moonlit valley below them stood the "ha'nted" house, utterly isolated, its fences gone long ago, rank weeds smothering the very doorsteps, the chimney crumbled to ruin, the window-sashes vacant, a corner of the roof caved in. The boys gazed awhile, half expecting to see a blue light flit past a window; then talking in a low tone, as befitted the time and the circumstances, they struck far off to the right, to give the haunted house a wide berth, and took their way homeward through the woods that adorned the rearward side of Cardiff Hill.

About noon the next day the boys arrived at the dead tree; they had come for their tools. Tom was impatient to go to the haunted house; Huck was measurably so, also—but suddenly said:

"Lookyhere, Tom, do you know what day it is?"

Tom mentally ran over the days of the week, and then quickly lifted his eyes with a startled look in them—

"My! I never once thought of it, Huck!"

"Well, I didn't neither, but all at once it popped onto me that it was Friday."

"Blame it, a body can't be too careful, Huck. We might 'a' got into an awful scrape, tackling such a thing on a Friday."

"*Might!* Better say we *would!* There's some lucky days, maybe, but Friday ain't."

"Any fool knows that. I don't reckon *you* was the first that found it out, Huck."

"Well, I never said I was, did I? And Friday ain't all, neither. I had a rotten bad dream last night—dreampt about rats."

"No! Sure sign of trouble. Did they fight?"

"No."

"Well, that's good, Huck. When they don't fight it's only a sign that there's trouble around, you know. All we got to do is to look mighty sharp and keep out of it. We'll drop this thing for today, and play. Do you know Robin Hood, Huck?"

"No. Who's Robin Hood?"

"Why, he was one of the greatest men that was ever in England— and the best. He was a robber."

"Cracky, I wisht I was. Who did he rob?"

"Only sheriffs and bishops and rich people and kings, and such like. But he never bothered the poor. He loved 'em. He always divided up with 'em perfectly square."

"Well, he must 'a' been a brick."

"I bet you he was, Huck. Oh, he was the noblest man that ever was. They ain't any such men now, I can tell you. He could lick any man in England, with one hand tied behind him; and he could take his yew bow and plug a ten-cent piece every time, a mile and a half."

"What's a *yew* bow?"

"I don't know. It's some kind of a bow, of course. And if he hit that dime only on the edge he would set down and cry—and curse. But we'll play Robin Hood—it's nobby fun. I'll learn you."

"I'm agreed."

So they played Robin Hood all the afternoon, now and then casting a yearning eye down upon the haunted house and passing a remark about the morrow's prospects and possibilities there. As the sun began to sink into the west they took their way homeward athwart the long shadows of the trees and soon were buried from sight in the forests of Cardiff Hill.

On Saturday, shortly after noon, the boys were at the dead tree again. They had a smoke and a chat in the shade, and then dug a little in their last hole, not with great hope, but merely because Tom said there were so many cases where people had given up a treasure after getting down within six inches of it, and then somebody else had come along and turned it up with a single thrust of a shovel. The thing failed this time, however, so the boys shouldered their tools and went away feeling that they had not trifled with fortune, but had fulfilled all the requirements that belong to the business of treasure-hunting.

When they reached the haunted house there was something so weird and grisly about the dead silence that reigned there under the baking sun, and something so depressing about the loneliness and desolation of the place, that they were afraid, for a moment, to venture in. Then they crept to the door and took a trembling peep. They saw a weedgrown, floorless room, unplastered, an ancient fireplace, vacant windows, a ruinous staircase; and here, there, and everywhere hung ragged and abandoned cobwebs. They presently entered, softly, with quickened pulses, talking in whispers, ears alert to catch the slightest sound, and muscles tense and ready for instant retreat.

In a little while familiarity modified their fears and they gave the place a critical and interested examination, rather admiring their own boldness, and wondering at it, too. Next they wanted to look upstairs. This was something like cutting off retreat, but they got to daring each other, and of course there could be but one result—they threw their tools into a corner and made the ascent. Up there were the same signs of decay. In one corner they found a closet that promised mystery, but the promise was a fraud—there was nothing in it. Their courage was up now and well in hand. They were about to go down and begin work when—

"Sh!" said Tom.

"What is it?" whispered Huck, blanching with fright.

"Sh! . . . There! . . . Hear it?"

"Yes! . . . Oh, my! Let's run!"

"Keep still! Don't you budge! They're coming right toward the door."

The boys stretched themselves upon the floor with their eyes to knotholes in the planking, and lay waiting, in a misery of fear.

"They've stopped. . . . No—coming. . . . Here they are. Don't whisper another word, Huck. My goodness, I wish I was out of this!"

Two men entered. Each boy said to himself: "There's the old deaf and dumb Spaniard that's been about town once or twice lately—never saw t'other man before."

"T'other" was a ragged, unkempt creature, with nothing very pleasant in his face. The Spaniard was wrapped in a serape; he had bushy white whiskers; long white hair flowed from under his sombrero, and he wore green goggles. When they came in, "t'other" was talking in a low voice; they sat down on the ground, facing the door, with their backs to the wall, and the speaker continued his remarks. His manner became less guarded and his words more distinct as he proceeded:

"No," said he, "I've thought it all over, and I don't like it. It's dangerous."

"Dangerous!" grunted the "deaf and dumb" Spaniard—to the vast surprise of the boys. "Milksop!"

This voice made the boys gasp and quake. It was Joe's! There was silence for some time. Then Joe said:

"What's any more dangerous than that job up yonder—but nothing's come of it."

"That's different. Away up the river so, and not another house about. 'Twon't ever be known that we tried, anyway, long as we didn't succeed."

"Well, what's more dangerous than coming here in the daytime!—anybody would suspicion us that saw us."

"I know that. But there warn't any other place as handy after that fool of a job. I want to quit this shanty. I wanted to yesterday, only it warn't any use trying to stir out of here, with those infernal boys playing over there on the hill right in full view."

"Those infernal boys" quaked again under the inspiration of this remark, and thought how lucky it was that they had remembered it was Friday and concluded to wait a day. They wished in their hearts they had waited a year.

The two men got out some food and made a luncheon. After a long and thoughtful silence, Joe said:

"Look here, lad—you go back up the river where you belong. Wait there till you hear from me. I'll take the chances on dropping into this town just once more, for a look. We'll do that 'dangerous' job after I've spied around a little and think things look well for it. Then for Texas! We'll leg it together!"

This was satisfactory. Both men presently fell to yawning, and Joe said:

"I'm dead for sleep! It's your turn to watch."

He curled down in the weeds and soon began to snore. His comrade stirred him once or twice and he became quiet. Presently the watcher began to nod; his head drooped lower and lower, both men began to snore now.

The boys drew a long, grateful breath. Tom whispered:

"Now's our chance—come!"

Huck said:

"I can't—I'd die if they was to wake."

Tom urged—Huck held back. At last Tom rose slowly and softly, and started alone. But the first step he made wrung such a hideous creak from the crazy floor that he sank down almost dead with fright. He never made a second attempt. The boys lay there counting the dragging moments till it seemed to them that time must be done and eternity growing gray; and then they were grateful to note that at last the sun was setting.

Now one snore ceased. Joe sat up, stared around—smiled grimly upon his comrade, whose head was drooping upon his knees—stirred him up with his foot and said:

"Here! *You're* a watchman, ain't you! All right, though—nothing's happened."

"My! have I been asleep?"

"Oh, partly, partly. Nearly time for us to be moving, pard. What'll we do with what little swag we've got left?"

"I don't know—leave it here as we've always done, I reckon. No use to take it away till we start south. Six hundred and fifty in silver's something to carry."

"Well—all right—it won't matter to come here once more."

"No—but I'd say come in the night as we used to do—it's better."

"Yes: but look here; it may be a good while before I get the right chance at that job; accidents might happen; 'tain't in such a very good place; we'll just regularly bury it—and bury it deep."

"Good idea," said the comrade, who walked across the room, knelt down, raised one of the rearward hearth-stones and took out a bag that jingled pleasantly. He subtracted from it twenty or thirty dollars for himself and as much for Joe, and passed the bag to the latter, who was on his knees in the corner, now, digging with his bowie-knife.

The boys forgot all their fears, all their miseries in an instant. With gloating eyes they watched every movement. Luck!—the splendor of it was beyond all imagination! Six hundred dollars was money enough to make half a dozen boys rich! Here was treasure-hunting under the happiest auspices—there would not be any bothersome uncertainty as to where to dig. They nudged each other every moment—eloquent nudges and easily understood, for they simply meant—"Oh, but ain't you glad *now* we're here!"

Joe's knife struck upon something.

"Hello!" said he.

"What is it?" said his comrade.

"Half-rotten plank—no, it's a box, I believe. Here—bear a hand and we'll see what it's here for. Never mind, I've broke a hole."

He reached his hand in and drew it out—

"Man, it's money!"

The two men examined the handful of coins. They were gold. The boys above were as excited as themselves, and as delighted.

Joe's comrade said:

"We'll make quick work of this. There's an old rusty pick over amongst the weeds in the corner the other side of the fireplace—I saw it a minute ago."

He ran and brought the boys' pick and shovel. Joe took the pick, looked it over critically, shook his head, muttered something to himself, and then began to use it. The box was soon unearthed. It was not very large; it was iron bound and had been very strong before the slow years had injured it. The men contemplated the treasure awhile in blissful silence.

"Pard, there's thousands of dollars here," said Joe.

"'Twas always said that Murrel's gang used to be around here one summer," the stranger observed.

"I know it," said Joe; "and this looks like it, I should say."

"Now you won't need to do that job."

The halfbreed frowned. Said he:

"You don't know me. Least you don't know all about that thing. 'Tain't robbery altogether—it's *revenge!*" and a wicked light flamed in his eyes. "I'll need your help in it. When it's finished—then Texas. Go home to your wife and your kids, and stand by till you hear from me."

"Well—if you say so; what'll we do with this—bury it again?"

"Yes. [Ravishing delight overhead.] *No!* by the great Sachem, no! [Profound distress overhead.] I'd nearly forgot. That pick had fresh earth on it! [The boys were sick with terror in a moment.] What business has a pick and a shovel here? What business with fresh earth on them? Who brought them here—and where are they gone? Have you heard anybody?—seen anybody? What! bury it again and leave them to come and see the ground disturbed? Not exactly—not exactly. We'll take it to my den."

"Why, of course! Might have thought of that before. You mean Number One?"

"No—Number Two—under the cross. The other place is bad—too common."

"All right. It's nearly dark enough to start."

Joe got up and went about from window to window cautiously peeping out. Presently he said:

"Who could have brought those tools here? Do you reckon they can be upstairs?"

The boys' breath forsook them. Joe put his hand on his knife, halted a moment, undecided, and then turned toward the stairway. The boys thought of the closet, but their strength was gone. The steps came creaking up the stairs—the intolerable distress of the situation woke the stricken resolution of the lads—they were about to spring for the closet, when there was a crash of rotten timbers and Joe landed on the ground amid the debris of the ruined stairway. He gathered himself up cursing, and his comrade said:

"Now what's the use of all that? If it's anybody, and they're up there, let them *stay* there—who cares? If they want to jump down, now, and get into trouble, who objects? It will be dark in fifteen minutes—and then let them follow us if they want to. I'm willing. In my opinion, whoever hove those things in here caught a sight of us and took us for ghosts or devils or something. I'll bet they're running yet."

Joe grumbled awhile; then he agreed with his friend that what daylight was left ought to be economized in getting things ready for leaving. Shortly afterward they slipped out of the house in the deepening twilight, and moved toward the river with their precious box.

Tom and Huck rose up, weak but vastly relieved, and stared after them through the chinks between the logs of the house. Follow? Not they. They were content to reach ground again without broken necks, and take the townward track over the hill. They did not talk much. They were too much absorbed in hating themselves—hating the ill luck that made them take the spade and the pick there. But for that, Joe never would have suspected. He would have hidden the silver with the gold to wait there till his "revenge" was satisfied, and then he would have had the misfortune to find that money turn up missing. Bitter, bitter luck that the tools were ever brought there!

They resolved to keep a lookout for that Spaniard when he should come to town spying out for chances to do his revengeful job, and follow him to "Number Two," wherever that might be. Then a ghastly thought occurred to Tom.

"Revenge? What if he means *us*, Huck!"

"Oh, don't!" said Huck, nearly fainting.

They talked it all over, and as they entered town they agreed to believe that he might possibly mean somebody else—at least that he might at least mean nobody but Tom, since only Tom had testified.

Very, very small comfort it was to Tom to be alone in danger! Company would be a palpable improvement, he thought.

6

BAD START AT DAWSON

BY W. H. P. JARVIS

Dawson City was the Klondike destination gold-seekers were desperate to reach in their gold rush quest. Located about 550 miles down the Yukon River from the trails and passes leading out of Skagway, Dawson was thought to be the center of goldfield operations. The journey there was physically difficult and dangerous. Once they reached Dawson, the prospectors expected to start reaping the gold of the dreams that had brought them there. What they found, however, was more work, more danger, and fading dreams.

Being in the vanguard of the multitude, whose rush to the diggings in the following year was the outstanding feature of the history of the Klondike, the Dawson that John Berwick and his companions found was that of the winter of '97, very different from the city of five thousand tents it was to become two months after their arrival!

An hour before midnight, when they arrived, Hugh had pointed out a high hill, Dawson's Dome, placed beyond the mouth of the Klondike River, or, as it was called before usage corrupted its name, the Thron Duik. Little did he or his companions dream of the part this Dome was to play in the events yet to be! The Dome was to become historic.

The main portion of Dawson was built on the north side of the Klondike. It was a scene of much movement and business. Pack-trains were passing up and down the streets, and innumerable dogs seemed everywhere.

Few boats had yet arrived, and a group of loafers gathered to watch them land. One fellow shouted, "I'll give you a dollar apiece for any late papers you have!"

Now that they were at the Klondike capital, the natural impulse of the party was to enjoy whatever amusements were available; so, in spite of their being tired, and the hour late, they drew the boat upon the gravel shore. Passing between tents, they came to the mire of the main thoroughfare. The atmosphere and circumstance of the gold-fields were all about them. There were pack-horses and pack-mules waiting before the shops. Men were hurrying in and out with pack-straps on their backs. Even the dogs wore saddle-bags—a good dog being able to pack forty pounds of supplies. Other dogs passed draw-ing a cart, on which were half-a-dozen cans, oil-tins filled with water, dispensed at twenty-five cents the tin.

The festive side of life was more marked than the commercial. Men in wild attire, women in gorgeous raiment, were ever passing in and out of the saloons and gambling-halls. The four adventurers floun-dered across the mud and entered the hospitable doors of the Borea-lis. This was a saloon and dance-hall combined; but a roulette-wheel and faro lay-out invited to play. It was the interval between the dances when they entered, and a loud voice was calling: "Come along, gen-tlemen, pretty ladies here!—just in over the ice. The next dance will be a waltz."

Frank Corte—ever the squire of dames—made a dive for the rear of the hall, and was soon leading one of the gorgeous creatures into the dizzy whirl. The partners from the last dance were crowding the bar, ordering drinks. As each man paid his two dollars his "lady" was handed a check. This check was redeemable for one dollar—the girls' source of revenue!

The orchestra was good, but the male section of the dancers was certainly grotesque; many of the men, with sombreros on their head and cigars between their teeth, were floundering through the dance in a half-intoxicated condition, their great hob-nailed boots almost drowning the music with their noise.

The three others soon left Frank to his diversions, and passed out to the street. They saw a policeman, with whom, in the way of such a free-and-easy community, they fell into talk.

"What's the chance of getting a claim?" they asked.

"Don't know. They are having stampedes right along, and any time you may hear of good pay being located on a creek. When news like this gets out there is a big rush by all classes, and you're lucky if you get anywhere near discovery. If you want work, they are paying ten dollars per day and board on the creeks for shovelling in—so I guess you need not starve!"

Hugh, with his mind on the immediate necessities of the party, asked, "Where is a good place to locate?"

"Up on the bench on the north side of the Klondike over there." The policeman pointed south-east. "You can get wood handy, and the water is good."

"What's the matter with pitching our tent where we landed?"

"Among the outfit along the water-front? No, they are the sore heads and general kickers. You don't want to tie to them. Most of them have lived in these tents all winter, and had nothing to do but dream of what some other fellow has done them out of, and how much better things would be if they had struck it rich instead of McDonald or Carmack! No, you fellows pole up-stream tomorrow to the Klondike, and then up that stream half a mile. Pack your grub to the top of the hill there, where you can live like white men."

"That sounds reasonable, but we want to sleep now."

"Well, go to Flanagan's bunk-house up the street," and the man pointed up a turning running at right angles to the main street. "He will give you beds at a dollar each."

"Our boat and things will be all right? Good-night—and thanks."

When the three visited the boat next morning they found a man standing on the bank, his legs—encased in rubber boots coming up to his
hips—far apart, hands in the pockets of his overalls, a sombrero on the
back of his head. Hugh noticed the smile of good-natured cynicism on
his face as he regarded the boat, and said, "Queer, ain't it? And they say
there are thousands more coming."

"Yes, fifty thousand more coming in—and me waiting for a chance
to get out!"

"I wonder what makes them do it?"

"Same thing as made me do it."

"Didn't you git a chance to stake anything?"

"Stake anything!—how long have you been in the country? Say! is
that your boat?"

"Yes."

"Well, take my tip and just get in it, and keep right on going till you
strike St. Michael's."

"For what reason would we do that?"

"Don't you know they have a Government in this country? Well,
that's the reason: officials and graft! Stake a claim, and they rob you
of it! No, sir, no more British mining-camps for me. I'm for the good
old State of Washington. If this camp was in Alaska a fellow could
hold down what was his with a shot-gun; but here you daren't make
a break. Law and order!—hell! Grafters appointed by the law, and the
law to see no fellow interfere with the grafters! We'd shoot the whole
bunch if we had them on the other side."

"We intend to stake claims, and we intend to hold them."

"You do, eh?—well, I bet you won't. You fellows should have
brought your nurse-girls with you to teach you the A B C."

The party was then joined by Frank, the habitual smile on his face; but his eyes were heavy.

"Cost me fifty dollars!" he said.

"You got off easy—better get in and cook breakfast to wake you up. We haven't eaten yet, and meals up town cost two dollars and a half!"

"Say! if you fellows want to you can use my tent and things, but I have no grub to give away."

This invitation from the new-found pessimist was accepted, and Frank went to work cooking while their host let loose his opinions upon life.

He told them how the manager of a great trading company had the autumn before addressed the crowd, prophesying famine through the winter and exhorting all to leave the place by the only avenue of escape—the river, then filling with ice. It was a dismal picture enough, but happily worse than the reality. He spoke well of the police, and praised the way they had rushed the mail in and out with dog-teams. "And it ain't their fault there is so much grafting; they don't graft themselves."

He told of the fabulous wealth of Eldorado, Bonanza, and Hunker Creeks, and of Alec McDonald, the "Big Moose," estimated to be worth $26,000,000. He expatiated at length upon the irregularities of the Gold Commissioner's office; the iniquitous Orders-in-Council from Ottawa, such as the imposition of ten per cent royalty on the production of the creeks, and the reserving to the Crown of every alternate claim on Dominion Creek, of all other creeks on which new discoveries might have been made, and of the hillside claims.

Frank, with his Yankee predilections, was ready to believe anything bad of Canada, and chuckled at the account. John and George, though they had had experience of official corruption in Australia, thought the accounts fantastic, and could not believe such things possible in British dominions. "The Gold Commissioner is not in the graft; he's honest—but he's like a baby, and the gang play with him as they like."

Breakfast over, the party set out, and in an hour had poled and tracked the boat half a mile up the Klondike. They passed under a crude suspension bridge and saw two ferries and innumerable boats plying across the river.

Hugh noticed a break or "draw" in the cliff, marked by a trail that led to the bench on which the party was to locate, and stopped the boat.

"Get out the axes, fellows; and, Frank, you pack the tent up the hill. It will make you think of what you have done with your last winter's wages. John, you're the honoured guest—you're going to boss the job."

Berwick, without any load, found the climb to the top of the hill sufficiently exhausting, as he was not yet fully recovered. After Frank had thrown down the tent Hugh unlashed it, and spread it in the sun, folded one end to make a pillow, and told John to lie upon it. And then he addressed his partners:

"Look here, fellows—one thing is certain. Whatever we do as regards prospecting and taking up claims, we want a home-camp as a sort of headquarters; and we might as well make it here and now. We need not bother building a cabin, but we can put up a wall of logs the size of the tent and put the tent on top. This will do till the fall, by which time we will all be millionaires—except Frank here, unless he quits dancing! Now we'll pack up the rest of the outfit. Come on, boys!"

By four o'clock their new habitation was completed: two beds were built and the little stove erected inside the tent. Frank had an early supper and went to bed. The others built a camp-fire outside to keep away the flies, and discussed mining far into the night.

7

TO BUILD A FIRE

BY JACK LONDON

Day had broken cold and gray, exceedingly cold and gray, when the man turned aside from the main Yukon trail and climbed the high earth-bank, where a dim and little-travelled trail led eastward through the fat spruce timberland. It was a steep bank, and he paused for breath at the top, excusing the act to himself by looking at his watch. It was nine o'clock. There was no sun nor hint of sun, though there was not a cloud in the sky. It was a clear day, and yet there seemed an intangible pall over the face of things, a subtle gloom that made the day dark, and that was due to the absence of sun. This fact did not worry the man. He was used to the lack of sun. It had been days since he had seen the sun, and he knew that a few more days must pass before that cheerful orb, due south, would just peep above the skyline and dip immediately from view.

The man flung a look back along the way he had come. The Yukon lay a mile wide and hidden under three feet of ice. On top of this ice were as many feet of snow. It was all pure white, rolling in gentle undulations where the ice jams of the freeze-up had formed. North and south, as far as his eye could see, it was unbroken white, save for a dark hairline that curved and twisted from around the spruce-covered island to the south, and that curved and twisted away into the north, where it disappeared behind another spruce-covered island. This dark hairline was the trail—the main trail—that led south five hundred miles to the Chilcoot Pass, Dyea, and salt water; and that led north seventy miles to Dawson, and still on to the north a thousand miles to Nulato, and finally to St. Michael, on Bering Sea, a thousand miles and half a thousand more.

But all this—this mysterious, far-reaching hairline trail, the absence of sun from the sky, the tremendous cold, and the strangeness and weirdness of it all—made no impression on the man. It was not because he was long used to it. He was a newcomer in the land, a *chechaquo*, and this was his first winter. The trouble with him was that he was without imagination. He was quick and alert in the things of life, but only in things, and not in the significances. Fifty degrees below zero meant eighty-odd degrees of frost. Such fact impressed him as being cold and uncomfortable, and that was all. It did not lead him to meditate upon his frailty as a creature of temperature, and upon man's frailty in general, able only to live within certain narrow limits of heat and cold; and from there on it did not lead him to the conjectural field of immortality and man's place in the universe. Fifty degrees below zero stood for a bite of frost that hurt and that must be guarded against by use of mittens, ear flaps, warm moccasins, and thick socks.

Fifty degrees below zero was to him just precisely fifty degrees below zero. That there should be anything more to it than that was a thought that never entered his head.

As he turned to go, he spat speculatively. There was a sharp, explosive crackle that startled him. He spat again. And again, in the air, before it could fall to the snow, the spittle crackled. He knew that at fifty below spittle crackled on the snow, but this spittle had crackled in the air. Undoubtedly it was colder than fifty below—how much colder he did not know. But the temperature did not matter. He was bound for the old claim on the left fork of Henderson Creek, where the boys were already. They had come over across the divide from the Indian Creek country, while he had come the roundabout way to take a look at the possibilities of getting out logs in the spring from the islands in the Yukon. He would be in to camp by six o'clock; a bit after dark, it was true, but the boys would be there, a fire would be going, and a hot supper would be ready. As for lunch, he pressed his hand against the protruding bundle under his jacket. It was also under his shirt, wrapped up in a handkerchief and lying against the naked skin. It was the only way to keep the biscuits from freezing. He smiled agreeably to himself as he thought of those biscuits, each cut open and sopped in bacon grease, and each enclosing a generous slice of fried bacon.

He plunged in among the big spruce trees. The trail was faint. A foot of snow had fallen since the last sled had passed over, and he was glad he was without a sled, travelling light. In fact, he carried nothing but the lunch wrapped in the handkerchief. He was surprised, however, at the cold. It certainly was cold, he concluded, as he rubbed his numb nose and cheekbones with his mittened hand. He was a warm-whiskered man, but the hair on his face did not protect the high cheekbones and the eager nose that thrust itself aggressively into the frosty air.

At the man's heels trotted a dog, a big native husky, the proper wolf dog, gray-coated and without any visible or temperamental difference from its brother, the wild wolf. The animal was depressed by the tremendous cold. It knew that it was no time for travelling. Its instinct told it a truer tale than was told to the man by the man's judgment. In reality, it was not merely colder than fifty below zero; it was colder than sixty below, than seventy below. It was seventy-five below zero. Since the freezing point is thirty-two above zero, it meant that one hundred and seven degrees of frost obtained. The dog did not know anything about thermometers. Possibly in its brain there was no sharp consciousness of a condition of very cold such as was in the man's brain. But the brute had its instinct. It experienced a vague but menacing apprehension that subdued it and made it slink along at the man's heels, and that made it question eagerly every unwonted movement of the man as if expecting him to go into camp or to seek shelter somewhere and build a fire. The dog had learned fire, and it wanted fire, or else to burrow under the snow and cuddle its warmth away from the air.

The frozen moisture of its breathing had settled on its fur in a fine powder of frost, and especially were its jowls, muzzle and eyelashes whitened by its crystalled breath. The man's red beard and mustache were likewise frosted, but more solidly, the deposit taking the form of ice and increasing with every warm, moist breath he exhaled. Also, the man was chewing tobacco, and the muzzle of ice held his lips so rigidly that he was unable to clear his chin when he expelled the juice. The result was that a crystal beard of the color and solidity of amber was increasing its length on his chin. If he fell down it would shatter itself, like glass, into brittle fragments. But he did not mind the appendage. It was the penalty all tobacco chewers paid in that country, and he had been out before in two cold snaps. They had not been so cold as this, but by the spirit thermometer at Sixty-Mile he knew that they had been registered at fifty below and at fifty-five.

He held on through the level stretch of woods for several miles, crossed a wide flat of cottongrass, and dropped down a bank to the frozen bed of a small stream. This was Henderson Creek, and he knew he was ten miles from the forks. He looked at his watch. It was ten o'clock. He was making four miles an hour, and he calculated that he would arrive at the forks at half-past twelve. He decided to celebrate that event by eating his lunch there.

The dog dropped in again at his heels, with a tail drooping discouragement, as the man swung along the creek bed. The furrow of the old sled trail was plainly visible, but a dozen inches of snow covered the marks of the last runners. In a month no man had come up or down that silent creek. The man held steadily on. He was not much given to thinking, and just then particularly he had nothing to think about save that he would eat lunch at the forks and that at six o'clock he would be in camp with the boys. There was nobody to talk to; and, had there been, speech would have been impossible because of the ice muzzle on his mouth. So he continued monotonously to chew tobacco and to increase the length of his amber beard.

Once in a while the thought reiterated itself that it was very cold and that he had never experienced such cold. As he walked along he rubbed his cheekbones and nose with the back of his mittened hand. He did this automatically, now and again changing hands. But, rub as he would, the instant he stopped his cheekbones went numb, and the following instant the end of his nose went numb. He was sure to frost his cheeks; he knew that, and experienced a pang of regret that he had not devised a nose strap of the sort Bud wore in cold snaps. Such a strap passed across the cheeks, as well, and saved them. But it didn't matter much, after all. What were frosted cheeks? A bit painful, that was all; they were never serious.

Empty as the man's mind was of thoughts, he was keenly observant, and he noticed the changes in the creek, the curves and bends and timber jams, and always he sharply noted where he placed his feet. Once, coming around a bend he shied abruptly, like a startled horse, curved away from the place where he had been walking, and retreated several paces back along the trail. The creek he knew was frozen clear to the bottom—no creek could contain water in that arctic winter— but he knew also that there were springs that bubbled out from the hillsides and ran along under the snow and on top the ice of the creek. He knew that the coldest snaps never froze these springs, and he knew likewise their danger. They were traps. They hid pools of water under the snow that might be three inches deep, or three feet. Sometimes a skin of ice half an inch thick covered them, and in turn was covered by the snow. Sometimes there were alternate layers of water and ice skin, so that when one broke through he kept on breaking through for a while, sometimes wetting himself to the waist.

That was why he had shied in such panic. He had felt the give under his feet and heard the crackle of a snow-hidden ice skin. And to get his feet wet in such a temperature meant trouble and danger. At the very least it meant delay, for he would be forced to stop and build a fire, and under its protection to bare his feet while he dried his socks and moccasins. He stood and studied the creek bed and its banks, and decided that the flow of water came from his right. He reflected awhile, rubbing his nose and cheeks, then skirted to the left, stepping gingerly and testing the footing for each step. Once clear of the danger, he took a fresh chew of tobacco and swung along at his four-mile gait.

In the course of the next two hours he came upon several similar traps. Usually the snow above the hidden pools had a sunken, candied appearance that advertised the danger. Once again, however, he had a close call; and once, suspecting danger, he compelled the dog to go on in front. The dog did not want to go. It hung back until the man shoved it forward, and then it went quickly across the white, unbroken surface. Suddenly it broke through, floundered to one side, and got away to firmer footing. It had wet its forefeet and legs, and almost immediately the water that clung to it turned to ice. It made quick efforts to lick the ice off its legs, then dropped down in the snow and began to bite out the ice that had formed between the toes. This was a matter of instinct. To permit the ice to remain would mean sore feet. It did not know this. It merely obeyed the mysterious prompting that arose from the deep crypts of its being. But the man knew, having achieved a judgment on the subject, and he removed the mitten from his right hand and helped tear out the ice particles. He did not expose his fingers more than a minute, and was astonished at the swift numbness that smote them. It certainly was cold. He pulled on the mitten hastily, and beat the hand savagely across his chest.

At twelve o'clock the day was at its brightest. Yet the sun was too far south on its winter journey to clear the horizon. The bulge of the earth intervened between it and Henderson Creek, where the man walked under a clear sky at noon and cast no shadow. At half-past twelve, to the minute, he arrived at the forks of the creek. He was pleased at the speed he had made. If he kept it up, he would certainly be with the boys by six. He unbuttoned his jacket and shirt and drew forth his lunch. The action consumed no more than a quarter of a minute, yet in that brief moment the numbness laid hold of the exposed fingers. He did not put the mitten on, but, instead, struck the fingers a dozen sharp smashes against his leg. Then he sat down on a snow-covered log to eat. The sting that followed upon the striking of his fingers against his leg ceased so quickly that he was startled.

He had had no chance to take a bite of biscuit. He struck the fingers repeatedly and returned them to the mitten, baring the other hand for the purpose of eating. He tried to take a mouthful, but the ice muzzle prevented. He had forgotten to build a fire and thaw out. He chuckled at his foolishness, and as he chuckled he noted the numbness creeping into the exposed fingers. Also, he noted that the stinging which had first come to his toes when he sat down was already passing away. He wondered whether the toes were warm or numb. He moved them inside the moccasins and decided that they were numb.

He pulled the mitten on hurriedly and stood up. He was a bit frightened. He stamped up and down until the stinging returned into the feet. It certainly was cold, was his thought. That man from Sulphur Creek had spoken the truth when telling how cold it sometimes got in the country. And he had laughed at him at the time! That showed one must not be too sure of things. There was no mistake about it, it *was* cold. He strode up and down, stamping his feet and threshing his arms, until reassured by the returning warmth. Then he got out matches and proceeded to make a fire. From the undergrowth, where high water of the previous spring had lodged a supply of seasoned twigs, he got his firewood. Working carefully from a small beginning, he soon had a roaring fire, over which he thawed the ice from his face and in the protection of which he ate his biscuits. For the moment the cold of space was outwitted. The dog took satisfaction in the fire, stretching out close enough for warmth and far enough away to escape being singed.

When the man had finished, he filled his pipe and took his comfortable time over a smoke, then he pulled on his mittens, settled the ear flaps of his cap firmly about his ears, and took the creek trail up the left fork. The dog was disappointed and yearned back towards the fire. This man did not know cold. Possibly all the generations of his ancestry had been ignorant of cold, of real cold, of cold one hundred and seven degrees below freezing point. But the dog knew; all its ancestry knew, and it had inherited the knowledge. And it knew that it was not good to walk abroad in such fearful cold. It was the time to lie snug in a hole in the snow and wait for a curtain of cloud to be drawn across the face of outer space whence this cold came. On the other hand, there was no keen intimacy between the dog and the man. The one was the toil slave of the other, and the only caresses it had ever received were the caresses of the whip lash and of harsh and menacing throat sounds that threatened the whip lash. So the dog made no effort to communicate its apprehension to the man. It was not concerned in the welfare of the man; it was for its own sake that it yearned back toward the fire. But the man whistled, and spoke to it with the sound of whip lashes, and the dog swung in at the man's heels and followed after.

The man took a chew of tobacco and proceeded to start a new amber beard. Also, his moist breath quickly powdered with white his mustache, eyebrows, and lashes. There did not seem to be so many springs on the left fork of the Henderson, and for half an hour the man saw no signs of any. And then it happened. At a place where there were no signs, where the soft, unbroken snow seemed to advertise solidity beneath, the man broke through. It was not deep. He wet himself half-way to the knees before he floundered out to the firm crust.

He was angry, and cursed his luck aloud. He had hoped to get into camp with the boys at six o'clock, and this would delay him an hour, for he would have to build a fire and dry out his footgear. This was imperative at that low temperature—he knew that much; and he turned aside to the bank, which he climbed. On top, tangled in the underbrush about the trunks of several small spruce trees, was a high-water deposit of dry firewood—sticks and twigs, principally, but also larger portions of seasoned branches and fine, dry, last year's grasses. He threw down several large pieces on top of the snow. This served for a foundation and prevented the young flame from drowning itself in the snow it otherwise would melt. The flame he got by touching a match to a small shred of birch bark that he took from his pocket. This burned even more readily than paper. Placing it on the foundation, he fed the young flame with wisps of dry grass and with the tiniest dry twigs.

He worked slowly and carefully, keenly aware of his danger. Gradually, as the flame grew stronger, he increased the size of the twigs with which he fed it. He squatted in the snow, pulling the twigs out from their entanglement in the brush and feeding directly to the flame. He knew there must be no failure. When it is seventy-five below zero, a man must not fail in his first attempt to build a fire—that is, if his feet are wet. If his feet are dry, and he fails, he can run along the trail for half a mile and restore his circulation. But the circulation of wet and freezing feet cannot be restored by running when it is seventy-five below. No matter how fast he runs, the wet feet will freeze the harder.

All this the man knew. The old-timer on Sulphur Creek had told him about it the previous fall, and now he was appreciating the advice. Already all sensation had gone out of his feet. To build the fire he had been forced to remove his mittens, and the fingers had quickly gone numb. His pace of four miles an hour had kept his heart pumping blood to the surface of his body and to all the extremities. But the instant he stopped, the action of the pump eased down. The cold of space smote the unprotected tip of the planet, and he, being on that unprotected tip, received the full force of the blow. The blood of his body recoiled before it. The blood was alive, like the dog, and like the dog it wanted to hide away and cover itself up from the fearful cold. So long as he walked four miles an hour, he pumped the blood, willy-nilly, to the surface; but now it ebbed away and sank down into the recesses of his body. The extremities were the first to feel its absence. His wet feet froze the faster, and his exposed fingers numbed the faster, though they had not yet begun to freeze. Nose and cheeks were already freezing, while the skin of all his body chilled as it lost its blood.

But he was safe. Toes and nose and cheeks would be only touched by the frost, for the fire was beginning to burn with strength. He was feeding it with twigs the size of his finger. In another minute he would be able to feed it with branches the size of his wrist, and then he could remove his wet footgear, and, while it dried, he could keep his naked feet warm by the fire, rubbing them at first, of course, with snow. The fire was a success. He was safe. He remembered the advice of the old-timer on Sulphur Creek, and smiled. The old-timer had been very serious in laying down the law that no man must travel alone in the Klondike after fifty below. Well, here he was; he had had the accident; he was alone; and he had saved himself. Those old-timers were rather womanish, some of them, he thought. All a man had to do was to keep his head, and he was all right. Any man who was a man could travel alone. But it was surprising, the rapidity with which his cheeks and nose were freezing. And he had not thought his fingers could go lifeless in so short a time. Lifeless they were, for he could scarcely make them move together to grip a twig, and they seemed remote from his body and from him. When he touched a twig, he had to look and see whether or not he had hold of it. The wires were pretty well down between him and his finger ends.

All of which counted for little. There was the fire, snapping and crackling and promising life with every dancing flame. He started to untie his moccasins. They were coated with ice; the thick German socks were like sheaths of iron halfway to the knees; and the moccasin strings were like rods of steel all twisted and knotted as by some conflagration. For a moment he tugged with his numb fingers, then, realizing the folly of it, he drew his sheath knife.

But before he could cut the strings, it happened. It was his own fault or, rather, his mistake. He should not have built the fire under the spruce tree. He should have built it in the open. But it had been easier to pull the twigs from the brush and drop them directly on the fire. Now the tree under which he had done this carried a weight of snow on its boughs. No wind had blown for weeks, and each bough was full freighted. Each time he had pulled a twig he had communicated a slight agitation to the tree—an imperceptible agitation, so far as he was concerned, but an agitation sufficient to bring about the disaster. High up in the tree one bough capsized its load of snow. This fell on the boughs beneath, capsizing them. This process continued, spreading out and involving the whole tree. It grew like an avalanche, and it descended upon the man and the fire, and the fire was blotted out! Where it had burned was a mantle of fresh and disordered snow.

The man was shocked. It was as though he had just heard his own sentence of death. For a moment he sat and stared at the spot where the fire had been. Then he grew very calm. Perhaps the old-timer on Sulphur Creek was right. If he had only had a trail mate he would have been in no danger now. The trail mate could have built the fire. Well, it was up to him to build the fire over again, and this second time there must be no failure. Even if he succeeded, he would most likely lose some toes. His feet must be badly frozen by now, and there would be some time before the second fire was ready.

Such were his thoughts, but he did not sit and think them. He was busy all the time they were passing through his mind. He made a new foundation for a fire, this time out in the open, where no treacherous tree could blot it out. Next he gathered dry grasses and tiny twigs from the high-water flotsam. He could not bring his fingers together to pull them out, but he was able to gather them by the handful. In this way he got many rotten twigs and bits of green moss that were undesirable, but it was the best he could do. He worked methodically, even collecting an armful of larger branches to be used later when the fire gathered strength. And all the while the dog sat and watched him, a certain wistfulness in its eyes, for it looked upon him as the fire provider, and the fire was slow in coming.

When all was ready, the man reached in his pocket for a second piece of birch bark. He knew the bark was there, and though he could not feel it with his fingers, he could hear its crisp rustling as he fumbled for it. Try as he would, he could not clutch hold of it. And all the time, in his consciousness, was the knowledge that each instant his feet were freezing. This thought tended to put him in a panic, but he fought against it and kept calm. He pulled on his mittens with his teeth, and threshed his arms back and forth, beating his hands with all his might against his sides. He did this sitting down, and he stood up to do it; and all the while the dog sat in the snow, its wolf brush of a tail curled around warmly over its forefeet, its sharp wolf ears pricked forward intently as it watched the man. And the man, as he beat and threshed with his arms and hands, felt a great surge of envy as he regarded the creature that was warm and secure in its natural covering.

After a time he was aware of the first faraway signals of sensations in his beaten fingers. The faint tingling grew stronger till it evolved into a stinging ache that was excruciating, but which the man hailed with satisfaction. He stripped the mitten from his right hand and fetched forth the birch bark. The exposed fingers were quickly going numb again. Next he brought out his bunch of sulphur matches. But the tremendous cold had already driven the life out of his fingers. In his effort to separate one match from the others, the whole bunch fell into the snow. He tried to pick it out of the snow, but failed. The dead fingers could neither clutch nor touch. He was very careful. He drove the thought of his freezing feet, and nose, and cheeks, out of his mind, devoting his whole soul to the matches. He watched, using the sense of vision in place of that of touch, and when he saw his fingers on each side the bunch, he closed them—that is, he willed to close them, for the wires were down, and the fingers did not obey. He pulled the mitten on the right hand, and beat it fiercely against his knee. Then, with both mittened hands, he scooped the bunch of matches, along with much snow, into his lap. Yet he was no better off.

After some manipulation he managed to get the bunch between the heels of his mittened hands. In this fashion he carried it to his mouth. The ice crackled and snapped when by a violent effort he opened his mouth. He drew the lower jaw in, curled the upper lip out of the way and scraped the bunch with his upper teeth in order to separate a match. He succeeded in getting one, which he dropped on his lap. He was no better off. He could not pick it up. Then he devised a way. He picked it up in his teeth and scratched it on his leg. Twenty times he scratched before he succeeded in lighting it. As it flamed he held it with his teeth to the birch bark. But the burning brimstone went up his nostrils and into his lungs, causing him to cough spasmodically. The match fell into the snow and went out.

The old-timer on Sulphur Creek was right, he thought in the moment of controlled despair that ensued: after fifty below, a man should travel with a partner. He beat his hands, but failed in exciting any sensation. Suddenly he bared both hands, removing the mittens with his teeth. He caught the whole bunch between the heels of his hands. His arm muscles not being frozen enabled him to press the hand heels tightly against the matches. Then he scratched the bunch along his leg. It flared into flame, seventy sulphur matches at once! There was no wind to blow them out. He kept his head to one side to escape the strangling fumes, and held the blazing bunch to the birch bark. As he so held it, he became aware of sensation in his hand. His flesh was burning. He could smell it. Deep down below the surface he could feel it. The sensation developed into pain that grew acute. And still he endured it, holding the flame of the matches clumsily to the bark that would not light readily because his own burning hands were in the way, absorbing most of the flame.

At last, when he could endure no more, he jerked his hands apart. The blazing matches fell sizzling into the snow, but the birch bark was alight. He began laying dry grasses and the tiniest twigs on the flame. He could not pick and choose, for he had to lift the fuel between the heels of his hands. Small pieces of rotten wood and green moss clung to the twigs, and he bit them off as well as he could with his teeth. He cherished the flame carefully and awkwardly. It meant life, and it must not perish. The withdrawal of blood from the surface of his body now made him begin to shiver, and he grew more awkward. A large piece of green moss fell squarely on the little fire. He tried to poke it out with his fingers, but his shivering frame made him poke too far, and he disrupted the nucleus of the little fire, the burning grasses and the tiny twigs separating and scattering. He tried to poke them together again, but in spite of the tenseness of the effort, his shivering got away with him, and the twigs were hopelessly scattered. Each twig gushed a puff of smoke and went out. The fire provider had failed. As he looked apathetically about him, his eyes chanced on the dog, sitting across the ruins of the fire from him, in the snow, making restless, hunching movements, slightly lifting one forefoot and then the other, shifting its weight back and forth on them with wistful eagerness.

The sight of the dog put a wild idea into his head. He remembered the tale of the man, caught in a blizzard, who killed a steer and crawled inside the carcass, and so was saved. He would kill the dog and bury his hands in the warm body until the numbness went out of them. Then he could build another fire. He spoke to the dog, calling it to him; but in his voice was a strange note of fear that frightened the animal, who had never known the man to speak in such a way before. Something was the matter, and its suspicious nature sensed danger—it knew not what danger, but somewhere, somehow, in its brain arose an apprehension of the man. It flattened its ears down at the sound of the man's voice, and its restless, hunching movements and the liftings and shiftings of its forefeet became more pronounced; but it would not come to the man. He got on his hands and knees and crawled toward the dog. This unusual posture again excited suspicion, and the animal sidled mincingly away.

The man sat up in the snow for a moment and struggled for calmness. Then he pulled on his mittens, by means of his teeth, and got upon his feet. He glanced down at first in order to assure himself that he was really standing up, for the absence of sensation in his feet left him unrelated to the earth. His erect position in itself started to drive the webs of suspicion from the dog's mind; and when he spoke peremptorily, with the sound of whip lashes in his voice, the dog rendered its customary allegiance and came to him. As it came within reaching distance, the man lost his control. His arms flashed out to the dog, and he experienced genuine surprise when he discovered that his hands could not clutch, that there was neither bend nor feeling in his fingers. He had forgotten for the moment that they were frozen and that they were freezing more and more. All this happened quickly, and before the animal could get away, he encircled its body with his arms. He sat down in the snow, and in this fashion held the dog, while it snarled and whined and struggled.

But it was all he could do, hold its body encircled in his arms and sit there. He realized that he could not kill the dog. There was no way to do it. With his helpless hands he could neither draw nor hold his sheath knife nor throttle the animal. He released it, and it plunged wildly away, with tail between its legs, and still snarling. It halted forty feet away and surveyed him curiously, with ears sharply pricked forward.

The man looked down at his hands in order to locate them, and found them hanging on the ends of his arms. It struck him as curious that one should have to use his eyes in order to find out where his hands were. He began threshing his arms back and forth, beating the mittened hands against his sides. He did this for five minutes, violently, and his heart pumped enough blood up to the surface to put a stop to his shivering. But no sensation was aroused in his hands. He had an impression that they hung like weights on the ends of his arms, but when he tried to run the impression down, he could not find it.

A certain fear of death, dull and oppressive, came to him. This fear quickly became poignant as he realized that it was no longer a mere matter of freezing his fingers and toes, or of losing his hands and feet, but that it was a matter of life and death with the chances against him. This threw him into a panic, and he turned and ran along the old, dim trail. The dog joined in behind and kept up with him. He ran blindly, without intention, in fear such as he had never known in his life. Slowly, as he plowed and floundered through the snow, he began to see things again—the banks of the creek, the old timber jams, the leafless aspens, and the sky. The running made him feel better. He did not shiver. Maybe, if he ran on, his feet would thaw out; and, anyway, if he ran far enough, he would reach camp and the boys. Without doubt he would lose some fingers and toes and some of his face; but the boys would take care of him, and save the rest of him when he got there. And at the same time there was another thought in his mind that said he would never get to the camp and the boys; that he would soon be stiff and dead. This thought he kept in the background and refused to consider. Sometimes it pushed itself forward and demanded to be heard, but he thrust it back and strove to think of other things.

It struck him as curious that he could run at all on feet so frozen that he could not feel them when they struck the earth and took the weight of his body. He seemed to himself to skim along above the surface, and to have no connection with the earth. Somewhere he had once seen a winged Mercury, and he wondered if Mercury felt as he felt when skimming over the earth.

His theory of running until he reached camp and the boys had one flaw in it: he lacked the endurance. Several times he stumbled, and finally he tottered, crumpled up, and fell. When he tried to rise, he failed. He must sit and rest, he decided, and next time he would merely walk and keep on going. As he sat and regained his breath, he noted that he was feeling quite warm and comfortable. He was not shivering, and it even seemed that a warm glow had come to his chest and trunk. And yet, when he touched his nose or cheeks, there was no sensation. Running would not thaw them out. Nor would it thaw out his hands and feet. Then the thought came to him that the frozen portions of his body must be extending. He tried to keep this thought down, to forget it, to think of something else; he was aware of the panicky feeling that it caused, and he was afraid of the panic. But the thought asserted itself, and persisted, until it produced a vision of his body totally frozen. This was too much, and he made another wild run along the trail. Once he slowed down to a walk, but the thought of the freezing extending itself made him run again.

And all the time the dog ran with him, at his heels. When he fell down a second time, it curled its tail over its forefeet and sat in front of him, facing him, curiously eager and intent. The warmth and security of the animal angered him, and he cursed it till it flattened down its ears appeasingly. This time the shivering came more quickly upon the man. He was losing in his battle with the frost. It was creeping into his body from all sides. The thought of it drove him on, but he ran no more than a hundred feet, when he staggered and pitched headlong. It was his last panic. When he had recovered his breath and control, he sat up and entertained in his mind the conception of meeting death with dignity. However, the conception did not come to him in such terms. His idea of it was that he had been making a fool of himself, running around like a chicken with its head cut off—such was the simile that occurred to him. Well, he was bound to freeze anyway, and he might as well take it decently. With this newfound peace of mind came the first glimmerings of drowsiness. A good idea, he thought, to sleep off to death. It was like taking an anesthetic. Freezing was not so bad as people thought. There were lots worse ways to die.

He pictured the boys finding his body the next day. Suddenly he found himself with them, coming along the trail and looking for himself. And, still with them, he came around a turn in the trail and found himself lying in the snow. He did not belong with himself any more, for even then he was out of himself, standing with the boys and looking at himself in the snow. It certainly was cold, was his thought. When he got back to the States he could tell the folks what real cold was. He drifted on from this to a vision of the old-timer on Sulphur Creek. He could see him quite clearly, warm and comfortable, and smoking a pipe.

"You were right, old hoss; you were right," the man mumbled to the old-timer of Sulphur Creek.

Then the man drowsed off into what seemed to him the most comfortable and satisfying sleep he had ever known. The dog sat facing him and waiting. The brief day drew to a close in a long, slow twilight. There were no signs of a fire to be made, and, besides, never in the dog's experience had it known a man to sit like that in the snow and make no fire. As the twilight drew on, its eager yearning for the fire mastered it, and with a great lifting and shifting of forefeet, it whined softly, then flattened its ears down in anticipation of being chidden by the man. But the man remained silent. Later the dog whined loudly. And still later it crept close to the man and caught the scent of death. This made the animal bristle and back away. A little longer it delayed, howling under the stars that leaped and danced and shone brightly in the cold sky. Then it turned and trotted up the trail in the direction of the camp it knew, where there were other food providers and fire providers.

8

TREASURE ISLAND

BY ROBERT LEWIS STEVENSON

Despite the sweat, blood, and grit inherent with treasure-hunting activity, the literature of the subject can sometimes be quite charming. One writer who always delivered that ingredient was Robert Lewis Stevenson (1850–1894). His Treasure Island *is a treasure-hunting classic, filled with colorful characters, maps of hiding places, and sea-worthy pirate adventures. This excerpt brings us the first two chapters of the book. While not revealing buried treasure and unraveling the plot, the prose here provides portraits of the main characters and hints of the action to come.*

Quire Trelawney, Dr. Livesey, and the rest of these gentlemen having asked me to write down the whole particulars about Treasure Island, from the beginning to the end, keeping nothing back but the bearings of the island, and that only because there is still treasure not yet lifted, I take up my pen in the year of grace 17__ and go back to the time when my father kept the Admiral Benbow inn and the brown old seaman with the sabre cut first took up his lodging under our roof.

I remember him as if it were yesterday, as he came plodding to the inn door, his sea-chest following behind him in a hand-barrow—a tall, strong, heavy, nut-brown man, his tarry pigtail falling over the shoulder of his soiled blue coat, his hands ragged and scarred, with black, broken nails, and the sabre cut across one cheek, a dirty, livid white. I remember him looking round the cove and whistling to himself as he did so, and then breaking out in that old sea-song that he sang so often afterwards:

> Fifteen men on the dead man's chest—
> Yo-ho-ho, and a bottle of rum!

in the high, old tottering voice that seemed to have been tuned and broken at the capstan bars. Then he rapped on the door with a bit of stick like a handspike that he carried, and when my father appeared, called roughly for a glass of rum. This, when it was brought to him, he drank slowly, like a connoisseur, lingering on the taste and still looking about him at the cliffs and up at our signboard.

"This is a handy cove," says he at length; "and a pleasant sittyated grog-shop. Much company, mate?"

My father told him no, very little company, the more was the pity.

"Well, then," said he, "this is the berth for me. Here you, matey," he cried to the man who trundled the barrow; "bring up alongside and help up my chest. I'll stay here a bit," he continued. "I'm a plain man; rum and bacon and eggs is what I want, and that head up there for to watch ships off. What you mought call me? You mought call me captain. Oh, I see what you're at—there"; and he threw down three or four gold pieces on the threshold. "You can tell me when I've worked through that," says he, looking as fierce as a commander.

And indeed bad as his clothes were and coarsely as he spoke, he had none of the appearance of a man who sailed before the mast, but seemed like a mate or skipper accustomed to be obeyed or to strike. The man who came with the barrow told us the mail had set him down the morning before at the Royal George, that he had inquired what inns there were along the coast, and hearing ours well spoken of, I suppose, and described as lonely, had chosen it from the others for his place of residence. And that was all we could learn of our guest.

He was a very silent man by custom. All day he hung round the cove or upon the cliffs with a brass telescope; all evening he sat in a corner of the parlour next the fire and drank rum and water very strong. Mostly he would not speak when spoken to, only look up sudden and fierce and blow through his nose like a fog-horn; and we and the people who came about our house soon learned to let him be. Every day when he came back from his stroll he would ask if any seafaring men had gone by along the road. At first we thought it was the want of company of his own kind that made him ask this question, but at last we began to see he was desirous to avoid them. When a seaman did put up at the Admiral Benbow (as now and then some did, making by the coast road for Bristol) he would look in at him through the curtained door before he entered the parlour; and he was always sure to be as silent as a mouse when any such was present. For me, at least, there was no secret about the matter, for I was, in a way, a sharer in his alarms. He had taken me aside one day and promised me a silver fourpenny on the first of every month if I would only keep my "weather-eye open for a seafaring man with one leg" and let him know the moment he appeared. Often enough when the first of the month came round and I applied to him for my wage, he would only blow through his nose at me and stare me down, but before the week was out he was sure to think better of it, bring me my fourpenny piece, and repeat his orders to look out for "the seafaring man with one leg."

How that personage haunted my dreams, I need scarcely tell you. On stormy nights, when the wind shook the four corners of the house and the surf roared along the cove and up the cliffs, I would see him in a thousand forms, and with a thousand diabolical expressions. Now the leg would be cut off at the knee, now at the hip; now he was a monstrous kind of a creature who had never had but the one leg, and that in the middle of his body. To see him leap and run and pursue me over hedge and ditch was the worst of nightmares. And altogether I paid pretty dear for my monthly fourpenny piece, in the shape of these abominable fancies.

But though I was so terrified by the idea of the seafaring man with one leg, I was far less afraid of the captain himself than anybody else who knew him. There were nights when he took a deal more rum and water than his head would carry; and then he would sometimes sit and sing his wicked, old, wild sea-songs, minding nobody; but sometimes he would call for glasses round and force all the trembling company to listen to his stories or bear a chorus to his singing. Often I have heard the house shaking with "Yo-ho-ho, and a bottle of rum," all the neighbours joining in for dear life, with the fear of death upon them, and each singing louder than the other to avoid remark. For in these fits he was the most overriding companion ever known; he would slap his hand on the table for silence all round; he would fly up in a passion of anger at a question, or sometimes because none was put, and so he judged the company was not following his story. Nor would he allow anyone to leave the inn till he had drunk himself sleepy and reeled off to bed.

His stories were what frightened people worst of all. Dreadful stories they were—about hanging, and walking the plank, and storms at sea, and the Dry Tortugas, and wild deeds and places on the Spanish Main. By his own account he must have lived his life among some of the wickedest men that God ever allowed upon the sea, and the language in which he told these stories shocked our plain country people almost as much as the crimes that he described. My father was always saying the inn would be ruined, for people would soon cease coming there to be tyrannized over and put down, and sent shivering to their beds; but I really believe his presence did us good. People were frightened at the time, but on looking back they rather liked it; it was a fine excitement in a quiet country life, and there was even a party of the younger men who pretended to admire him, calling him a "true sea-dog" and a "real old salt" and such like names, and saying there was the sort of man that made England terrible at sea.

In one way, indeed, he bade fair to ruin us, for he kept on staying week after week, and at last month after month, so that all the money had been long exhausted, and still my father never plucked up the heart to insist on having more. If ever he mentioned it, the captain blew through his nose so loudly that you might say he roared, and stared my poor father out of the room. I have seen him wringing his hands after such a rebuff, and I am sure the annoyance and the terror he lived in must have greatly hastened his early and unhappy death.

All the time he lived with us the captain made no change whatever in his dress but to buy some stockings from a hawker. One of the cocks of his hat having fallen down, he let it hang from that day forth, though it was a great annoyance when it blew. I remember the appearance of his coat, which he patched himself upstairs in his room, and which, before the end, was nothing but patches. He never wrote or received a letter, and he never spoke with any but the neighbours, and with these, for the most part, only when drunk on rum. The great sea-chest none of us had ever seen open.

He was only once crossed, and that was towards the end, when my poor father was far gone in a decline that took him off. Dr. Livesey came late one afternoon to see the patient, took a bit of dinner from my mother, and went into the parlour to smoke a pipe until his horse should come down from the hamlet, for we had no stabling at the old Benbow. I followed him in, and I remember observing the contrast the neat, bright doctor, with his powder as white as snow and his bright, black eyes and pleasant manners, made with the coltish country folk, and above all, with that filthy, heavy, bleared scarecrow of a pirate of ours, sitting, far gone in rum, with his arms on the table. Suddenly he—the captain, that is—began to pipe up his eternal song:

Fifteen men on the dead man's chest—
Yo-ho-ho, and a bottle of rum!
Drink and the devil had done for the rest—
Yo-ho-ho, and a bottle of rum!

At first I had supposed "the dead man's chest" to be that identical big box of his upstairs in the front room, and the thought had been mingled in my nightmares with that of the one-legged seafaring man. But by this time we had all long ceased to pay any particular notice to the song; it was new, that night, to nobody but Dr. Livesey, and on him I observed it did not produce an agreeable effect, for he looked up for a moment quite angrily before he went on with his talk to old Taylor, the gardener, on a new cure for the rheumatics. In the meantime, the captain gradually brightened up at his own music, and at last flapped his hand upon the table before him in a way we all knew to mean silence. The voices stopped at once, all but Dr. Livesey's; he went on as before speaking clear and kind and drawing briskly at his pipe between every word or two. The captain glared at him for a while, flapped his hand again, glared still harder, and at last broke out with a villainous, low oath, "Silence, there, between decks!"

"Were you addressing me, sir?" says the doctor; and when the ruffian had told him, with another oath, that this was so, "I have only one thing to say to you, sir," replies the doctor, "that if you keep on drinking rum, the world will soon be quit of a very dirty scoundrel!"

The old fellow's fury was awful. He sprang to his feet, drew and opened a sailor's clasp-knife, and balancing it open on the palm of his hand, threatened to pin the doctor to the wall.

The doctor never so much as moved. He spoke to him as before, over his shoulder and in the same tone of voice, rather high, so that all the room might hear, but perfectly calm and steady: "If you do not put that knife this instant in your pocket, I promise, upon my honour, you shall hang at the next assizes."

Then followed a battle of looks between them, but the captain soon knuckled under, put up his weapon, and resumed his seat, grumbling like a beaten dog.

"And now, sir," continued the doctor, "since I now know there's such a fellow in my district, you may count I'll have an eye upon you day and night. I'm not a doctor only; I'm a magistrate; and if I catch a breath of complaint against you, if it's only for a piece of incivility like tonight's, I'll take effectual means to have you hunted down and routed out of this. Let that suffice."

Soon after, Dr. Livesey's horse came to the door and he rode away, but the captain held his peace that evening, and for many evenings to come.

T'was not very long after this that there occurred the first of the mysterious events that rid us at last of the captain, though not, as you will see, of his affairs. It was a bitter cold winter, with long, hard frosts and heavy gales; and it was plain from the first that my poor father was little likely to see the spring. He sank daily, and my mother and I had all the inn upon our hands, and were kept busy enough without paying much regard to our unpleasant guest.

It was one January morning, very early—a pinching, frosty morning—the cove all gray with hoar-frost, the ripple lapping softly on the stones, the sun still low and only touching the hilltops and shining far to seaward. The captain had risen earlier than usual and set out down the beach, his cutlass swinging under the broad skirts of the old blue coat, his brass telescope under his arm, his hat tilted back upon his head. I remember his breath hanging like smoke in his wake as he strode off, and the last sound I heard of him as he turned the big rock was a loud snort of indignation, as though his mind was still running upon Dr. Livesey.

Well, mother was upstairs with father and I was laying the breakfast-table against the captain's return when the parlour door opened and a man stepped in on whom I had never set my eyes before. He was a pale, tallowy creature, wanting two fingers of the left hand, and though he wore a cutlass, he did not look much like a fighter. I had always my eye open for seafaring men, with one leg or two, and I remember this one puzzled me. He was not sailorly, and yet he had a smack of the sea about him too.

I asked him what was for his service, and he said he would take rum; but as I was going out of the room to fetch it, he sat down upon a table and motioned me to draw near. I paused where I was, with my napkin in my hand.

"Come here, sonny," says he. "Come nearer here."

I took a step nearer.

"Is this here table for my mate Bill?" he asked with a kind of leer.

I told him I did not know his mate Bill, and this was for a person who stayed in our house whom we called the captain.

"Well," said he, "my mate Bill would be called the captain, as like as not. He has a cut on one cheek and a mighty pleasant way with him, particularly in drink, has my mate Bill. We'll put it, for argument like, that your captain has a cut on one cheek—and we'll put it, if you like, that that cheek's the right one. Ah, well! I told you. Now, is my mate Bill in this here house?"

I told him he was out walking.

"Which way, sonny? Which way is he gone?"

And when I had pointed out the rock and told him how the captain was likely to return, and how soon, and answered a few other questions, "Ah," said he, "this'll be as good as drink to my mate Bill."

The expression of his face as he said these words was not at all pleasant, and I had my own reasons for thinking that the stranger was mistaken, even supposing he meant what he said. But it was no affair of mine, I thought; and besides, it was difficult to know what to do. The stranger kept hanging about just inside the inn door, peering round the corner like a cat waiting for a mouse. Once I stepped out myself into the road, but he immediately called me back, and as I did not obey quick enough for his fancy, a most horrible change came over his tallowy face, and he ordered me in with an oath that made me jump. As soon as I was back again he returned to his former manner, half fawning, half sneering, patted me on the shoulder, told me I was a good boy and he had taken quite a fancy to me. "I have a son of my own," said he, "as like you as two blocks, and he's all the pride of my 'art. But the great thing for boys is discipline, sonny—discipline. Now, if you had sailed along of Bill, you wouldn't have stood there to be spoke to twice—not you. That was never Bill's way, nor the way of sich as sailed with him. And here, sure enough, is my mate Bill, with a spy-glass under his arm, bless his old 'art, to be sure. You and me'll just go back into the parlour, sonny, and get behind the door, and we'll give Bill a little surprise—bless his 'art, I say again."

So saying, the stranger backed along with me into the parlour and put me behind him in the corner so that we were both hidden by the open door. I was very uneasy and alarmed, as you may fancy, and it rather added to my fears to observe that the stranger was certainly frightened himself. He cleared the hilt of his cutlass and loosened the blade in the sheath; and all the time we were waiting there he kept swallowing as if he felt what we used to call a lump in the throat.

At last in strode the captain, slammed the door behind him, without looking to the right or left, and marched straight across the room to where his breakfast awaited him.

"Bill," said the stranger in a voice that I thought he had tried to make bold and big.

The captain spun round on his heel and fronted us; all the brown had gone out of his face, and even his nose was blue; he had the look of a man who sees a ghost, or the evil one, or something worse, if anything can be; and upon my word, I felt sorry to see him all in a moment turn so old and sick.

"Come, Bill, you know me; you know an old shipmate, Bill, surely," said the stranger.

The captain made a sort of gasp.

"Black Dog!" said he.

"And who else?" returned the other, getting more at his ease. "Black Dog as ever was, come for to see his old shipmate Billy, at the Admiral Benbow inn. Ah, Bill, Bill, we have seen a sight of times, us two, since I lost them two talons," holding up his mutilated hand.

"Now, look here," said the captain; "you've run me down; here I am; well, then, speak up; what is it?"

"That's you, Bill," returned Black Dog, "you're in the right of it, Billy. I'll have a glass of rum from this dear child here, as I've took such a liking to; and we'll sit down, if you please, and talk square, like old shipmates."

When I returned with the rum, they were already seated on either side of the captain's breakfast-table—Black Dog next to the door and sitting sideways so as to have one eye on his old shipmate and one, as I thought, on his retreat.

He bade me go and leave the door wide open. "None of your key-holes for me, sonny," he said; and I left them together and retired into the bar.

For a long time, though I certainly did my best to listen, I could hear nothing but a low gattling; but at last the voices began to grow higher, and I could pick up a word or two, mostly oaths, from the captain.

"No, no, no, no; and an end of it!" he cried once. And again, "If it comes to swinging, swing all, say I."

Then all of a sudden there was a tremendous explosion of oaths and other noises—the chair and table went over in a lump, a clash of steel followed, and then a cry of pain, and the next instant I saw Black Dog in full flight, and the captain hotly pursuing, both with drawn cutlasses, and the former streaming blood from the left shoulder. Just at the door the captain aimed at the fugitive one last tremendous cut, which would certainly have split him to the chine had it not been intercepted by our big signboard of Admiral Benbow. You may see the notch on the lower side of the frame to this day.

That blow was the last of the battle. Once out upon the road, Black Dog, in spite of his wound, showed a wonderful clean pair of heels and disappeared over the edge of the hill in half a minute. The captain, for his part, stood staring at the signboard like a bewildered man. Then he passed his hand over his eyes several times and at last turned back into the house.

"Jim," says he, "rum"; and as he spoke, he reeled a little, and caught himself with one hand against the wall.

"Are you hurt?" cried I.

"Rum," he repeated. "I must get away from here. Rum! Rum!"

I ran to fetch it, but I was quite unsteadied by all that had fallen out, and I broke one glass and fouled the tap, and while I was still getting in my own way, I heard a loud fall in the parlour, and running in, beheld the captain lying full length upon the floor. At the same instant my mother, alarmed by the cries and fighting, came running downstairs to help me. Between us we raised his head. He was breathing very loud and hard, but his eyes were closed and his face a horrible colour.

"Dear, deary me," cried my mother, "what a disgrace upon the house! And your poor father sick!"

In the meantime, we had no idea what to do to help the captain, nor any other thought but that he had got his death-hurt in the scuffle with the stranger. I got the rum, to be sure, and tried to put it down his throat, but his teeth were tightly shut and his jaws as strong as iron. It was a happy relief for us when the door opened and Doctor Livesey came in, on his visit to my father.

"Oh, doctor," we cried, "what shall we do? Where is he wounded?"

"Wounded? A fiddle-stick's end!" said the doctor. "No more wounded than you or I. The man has had a stroke, as I warned him. Now, Mrs. Hawkins, just you run upstairs to your husband and tell him, if possible, nothing about it. For my part, I must do my best to save this fellow's trebly worthless life; Jim, you get me a basin."

When I got back with the basin, the doctor had already ripped up the captain's sleeve and exposed his great sinewy arm. It was tattooed in several places. "Here's luck," "A fair wind," and "Billy Bones his fancy," were very neatly and clearly executed on the forearm; and up near the shoulder there was a sketch of a gallows and a man hanging from it—done, as I thought, with great spirit.

"Prophetic," said the doctor, touching this picture with his finger. "And now, Master Billy Bones, if that be your name, we'll have a look at the colour of your blood. Jim," he said, "are you afraid of blood?"

"No, sir," said I.

"Well, then," said he, "you hold the basin"; and with that he took his lancet and opened a vein.

A great deal of blood was taken before the captain opened his eyes and looked mistily about him. First he recognized the doctor with an unmistakable frown; then his glance fell upon me, and he looked relieved. But suddenly his colour changed, and he tried to raise himself, crying, "Where's Black Dog?"

"There is no Black Dog here," said the doctor, "except what you have on your own back. You have been drinking rum; you have had a stroke, precisely as I told you; and I have just, very much against my own will, dragged you headforemost out of the grave. Now, Mr. Bones—"

"That's not my name," he interrupted.

"Much I care," returned the doctor. "It's the name of a buccaneer of my acquaintance; and I call you by it for the sake of shortness, and what I have to say to you is this; one glass of rum won't kill you, but if you take one you'll take another and another, and I stake my wig if you don't break off short, you'll die—do you understand that?—die, and go to your own place, like the man in the Bible. Come, now, make an effort. I'll help you to your bed for once."

Between us, with much trouble, we managed to hoist him upstairs, and laid him on his bed, where his head fell back on the pillow as if he were almost fainting.

"Now, mind you," said the doctor, "I clear my conscience—the name of rum for you is death."

And with that he went off to see my father, taking me with him by the arm.

"This is nothing," he said as soon as he had closed the door. "I have drawn blood enough to keep him quiet awhile; he should lie for a week where he is—that is the best thing for him and you; but another stroke would settle him."

9

CALIFORNIA GOLD RUSH

BY CAPTAIN F. S. BERETON

When gold was discovered at Sutter's Mill in Coloma, California, in 1848, almost fifty years before the Klondike Gold Rush of 1897, cries of "Gold!" brought some 300,000 people. Though California was still two years from becoming a state, the California Territory was a destination with irresistible appeal and unappreciated dangers.

The gold rush to California was no new thing when Jack and his friends crossed the craggy heights of Nevada, and reached the green valleys to the west. Indeed it was already some years since the first of that long stream of eager individuals had pushed across the plains with the object of discovering gold. Some had made huge fortunes, many had made simply a living, while not a few had failed miserably.

"And a tidy sight of the poor things has left their bones out on them plains," said Tom, when discussing the matter. "I mind the time when America went mad about this here gold rush. Everyone was fer throwin' up a good and steady job, and ample wages, ter get over to Californy and try his luck. And in the minin' camps yer could meet the hard-working navvy, the store clerk, the doctor, the lawyer, and a host of others. There war men who had lost their all way back east, and fer whom the finding of gold meant everything. Mostly they was disappointed, 'cos gold diggin' aer a gamble, and gamblin' aer a game that ain't never safe ter play unless yer kin afford ter lose. Even then it ain't good. A man was meant ter take up a settled job, and put his back into it. Gamblers hope ter make a pile and live easy on it fer a time without troublin' to work. Wall, that ain't right. Men like that ain't much good ter their country."

"Hear, hear!" called out Steve.

"Yer see," went on Tom, "me and Steve was hunters first, and hun-tin' ain't a steady job, as it war. It includes makin' money as best we could, and it so happened that him and me was Californy way at the very right moment. We struck up pals, and went into partnership, and thar yer are. Wall, as I was sayin', yer could meet most any sort of man at the diggin's. The cut-throat and robber, as wasn't much good ter no one. The foreigner, the English gentleman, sailors and soldiers. Some came across the plains. A tidy few crossed Panama, and took ship ter 'Frisco. And thar they war, diggin' fer their lives, lookin' cross-eyed at their neighbours, lest they should strike a pile fust. This here Cali-forny's chock-full of minin' camps that's been abandoned and worked out. All them diggers settled on the easiest and most likely spots, and yer may take it that they've cleared the gold most everywhar whar it war easy ter get at. It ain't no longer any use comin' along and stakin' claims and workin' 'em. Ye've got ter prospect a heap, and then set up a plant bigger than any of them first diggers had."

"And ye've got ter settle down ter hard work," burst in Jacob.

"Ye have that," agreed Tom. "What do yer boys thar think of doin'? Me and Steve and Jack thar aer partners, as yer all know. We've lumped in a goodish sight of money, and we've got sufficient plant ter tackle any job. But we shall be wantin' labor."

"And six men ain't too many," said Steve quickly, lookin' across at Jacob.

Tom and Steve and Jack had talked the matter over on the previous day, and it had been agreed amongst them that they should invite the six scouts who had accompanied them across the plains to become their partners.

"Yer see," said Steve, when broaching the matter to Tom and our hero, "'tain't like takin' on men as we don't know. Jacob and the other boys has proved themselves real pals, and we kin trust 'em. It would pay us all ter go on as we aer."

"Look here, boys," cried Tom, facing the six men, "me and my mates has been having a jaw, and we decided we'd get to and ax yer ter come in along with us. We want help, willing help, and guess yer want work. Wall, now, there's seventeen Indian hosses, and away here in Californy horse flesh is mighty scarce jest now, and hard ter get. Ef we sold 'em we should make a fine lot of dollars, 'specially ef we didn't do a deal in too great a hurry. I mean, we could sell one here, another thar, and so on, gettin' good prices all the time. Then, once we've located a spot as seems likely, we kin get to and sell some of the team. Our saddle hosses kin pull the cart later on, if it aer needed ter get moved. Yer share of them seventeen hosses would give yer a little bit to put into the partnership. We'd pay yer so much wages ef yer didn't like that arrangement. But seems to me yer could each buy an interest. Then we all work fer the common good. Ef it pans out rich, we share according to the interest each man has. Ef we strike a bad egg, wall—"

"Yer try and try agin," laughed Jacob. "Now, look ye here, Tom, and you, Steve, and that 'ere Carrots. We've took to yer proper. There ain't been a sore word among us these past months. Wall, nat'ral like, we've been wonderin' what we'd do once we struck Californy. We aer here fer diggin', and sence ye're the same, why, we kinder estimated as ye'd be axin' us this question. We aer ready ter come in on these terms, and we think the offer handsome. Rightly, sence this here outfit aer yourn, them hosses we took from the Injuns aer yourn also. But sence you'll divide square, why, that aer a good sign that we'll get on friendly in this new venture. Me and my mates'll stand in ter win or lose. Seems ter me, seein' as we have some dollars ter work on, and needn't therefore rush at the job, as we stand an uncommon good chance."

It took but a little time to complete the arrangements, and accordingly the little party halted outside the first town they came to, where a lawyer drew up the proper agreements. Meanwhile a purchaser had been found for the Indian horses, which fetched a good price, and the share that Jacob and his five friends obtained allowed of their buying quite a respectable interest in the firm, though they would not, of course, have such a large interest as was held by Tom and Steve and Jack. A couple of days later they shook the dust of the town from their feet, and, with their cart replenished with sugar, flour, and other simple necessaries, took to the road again.

"There aer a gulch as me and Tom spotted last time we was over here," said Steve that evening. "We allowed as we'd make fer it when we came here agin, fer it promises somethin'. It aer been clean worked out in the flats by diggers."

"But that don't say as there ain't gold left," added Tom. "You, mates, haven't no experience of diggin', it seems, and so I'll tell yer a bit about it. Reckon gold aer been washin' outer the rocks of the mountains hereabouts fer centuries. It has got floated along in the streams, and where they run swift it hasn't settled. But as soon as ever it has reached a spot where the ground is flat, them 'ere specks of gold has come down to the bottom. In course of ages, what with dirt and gravel and sichlike, the bed of the river aer got filled bung up, and the water aer made a different course. Diggers has staked claims whar thar's been some old river bed, and have dug the gold from the gravel. They've took pretty well every ounce by now from sich sort of places; but they ain't by a long chalk got all the dust thar is in this country. Steve and me struck a gulch that seemed likely, and we're goin' thar to prospect."

It took the party another three weeks to find and reach the gulch of which Steve had spoken, and, once arrived, they set about prospecting in earnest for gold.

"Yer can see whar the old diggers came and dug their claims," explained Steve to Jack. "Everywhar down in the flats thar's holes and heaps of dirt. But none of them seed what Tom and me did. This gulch is narrow and flat; the sides come in suddenly, and rise to somewheres about four hundred feet. And up thar there's a big kind of tableland that runs back fer miles. Wall, now, the stream that come into the gulch back in them early times aer moved, else the miners wouldn't have been able ter stake their claims. Yer can't see it now, but ef yer ride ten miles up the gulch ye'll find it pouring over a cliff and crashin' down ter the bottom. Do yer see what I'm drivin' at?"

Jack thought he did. "I suppose your idea is to find the old stream, or the place where it once entered the gulch. I should say that if the land up there is flat, and the river shifted years and years ago to some other place, it must be because the bed up there got filled with gravel and stuff, and so deflected the course of the water."

"Right! That aer the thing that happened, I guess. Wall, now, we've got ter find the spot whar that 'ere stream tumbled over the cliff, and ter do that we don't need ter ride clear up the gulch and search all along. Them old miners are done that. Their diggin's don't go more than three miles up from here, and, as ye've seen fer yerself, there ain't any down lower. So I reckon that stream came over the cliff somewhars along these three miles. It may have been down here, or mebbe it war up thar. Thar ain't no sayin', and it ain't of no use ter go by the fall of the land.

Thar's been earthquakes and queer ructions here in past days, and the land aer altered."

It took a week's patient and careful scrutiny of the gulch to discover the point where the stream must have flowed into the gulch in past ages, and when the place was found, to the amazement of all it was almost precisely where they had made their temporary camp.

"Which aer a good omen," observed Jacob.

"Thet water must have been comin' over fer a sight of years," said Tom, as he clambered with Jack up the steep face of the cliff. "A chap might hunt and hunt, and never have no notion that it war here it come over. But a spade helps a deal in these matters, and here we have a solid stretch of gravel, sixty yards across, roughly, wedged in between a couple of rocky walls. Do yer foller what happened?"

"I think I see clearly," said Jack. "There must have been a deep slit in the rocks years ago, and the water flowed along it and emptied into this gulch. I suppose the water drained from mountains right over there?"

"That aer so," agreed Tom. "Thar's a big watershed back away at the top of the cliff, and thar must have been a flood coming along this channel."

"Slowly, I think," said Jack, "else the channel would have been continually washed clean. But it has filled and filled, till, in the course of ages, the whole thing has become blocked and the water has found a new channel for itself."

"And aer left us here a pile of gravel, which may or may not hold gold. Reckon, seein' that thim diggin's down thar is extensive and deep dug, that the miners in this camp made something of it. So thar's every chance that gold did come down. Ef it did, thar's a sight of it in this gravel. Not here, perhaps, for the stream would quicken a bit, just whar it was goin' ter fall; but a few yards back. Anyway, we'll set to and test it."

That afternoon picks and spades were hard at work on the wedge of gravel between its rocky walls. A cradle made of sheet iron was filled and taken down to the stream which passed the camp down below, and water was allowed to flow into it while Steve and Tom rocked it. Thar were anxious faces peering into the depths of the cradle, when at length the contents had been sufficiently washed. The water was allowed to drain away, big pieces of rock and stone were carefully removed, and finally a layer of sand was come upon. It glistened in the sun.

"Hooroo!" shouted Tom. "That aer gold. Not a heap of it, but gold; and tidy rich, I should say, seein' it comes from the face of the gravel. Now we'll take another sample."

They worked till night fell, and again on the following day. Choosing the very centre of the wedge of gravel, they burrowed some three yards into it, testing samples from time to time, and finding a richer deposit of gold dust in the cradle the deeper they went. Then, with a shout of satisfaction, Jacob unearthed a nugget the size of a bean.

"There ain't no need ter go farther," said Tom, when the night had fallen, and they were seated round the camp fire. "Thar aer work here fer the crowd of us ter take us a hull year. Now we has to engineer the business properly, fer it stands ter reason nine men, nor ninety, can't dig all that stuff away. It would take years. We have ter make some other sorter arrangement, and fer that we've the apparatus in the cart. What we'll do is this. We'll tap the river 'way up thar. Me and Steve measured it up yesterday: it aer jest twenty-eight yards from the edge, and out of line of the old stream. Perhaps it was formed only lately; but it carries heaps of water and will give us all we want. We'll lead it down through a wooden sluice, take the water ter an iron nozzle, and wash the dirt out into a wooden trough below. Now, mates, we want wood first of all, and some of us'll have ter get off ter the nearest sawmill ter buy and fetch it. T'others can fix the camp while they're gone, and get ter work diggin' the new channel up thar."

The whole plan of operations was quickly agreed upon, and promptly, on the following morning, Jacob and three of his mates unloaded the wagon, and went off with a full team to the sawmill, some twenty miles away. The others clambered to the top of the cliff, and for three days labored at digging a trench three feet wide and as many deep. They brought it from the bank of the stream mentioned by Tom which ran across the height above within reach of the edge, to the point where one of the rocky walls that had once enclosed the stream cropped into the open. Then they searched for a bed of clay, and finding some, puddled it with water till it was thin enough for their purpose, when they smeared it over the sides and bottom of the channel they had dug.

"It'll dry hard by to-morrow," said Tom; "then we'll give it another coat. It'll keep the water from washin' stones down into the nozzle and blockin' it. Jack, reckon the time's come fer yer anvil."

For the week following Jack found his hands filled. Up at cockcrow in the morning, he donned his leathern apron, and set his fire going. Then his hammer fell and clinked musically as he forged stout iron bands, which were to support the wooden framing his friends were constructing. It cost a great deal of hard labor to bring all their arrangements to a satisfactory completion; but when the task was finished they had a channel completed above, with a sluice by means of which they could allow water to enter at will. Another blocked the stream which they were tapping, just below their channel, thus giving them an ample head of water. The other end of the channel, where it ended at the edge of the cliff, was completely boxed in with boards, held together with heavy forgings, and from this point the water poured down a long, square wooden pipe, strengthened in the same manner.

At the very end the stream was led into a huge iron pipe, which got smaller and smaller, till it eventually presented a six-inch orifice, while the last six feet were capable of some amount of movement, whereby the course of the jet could be deflected.

"A man couldn't stand before it," said Tom, surveying the jet when all was ready. "The force of water'll be sich that ef we was ter close the jet it'd bust the wooden pipe above. As it is, thar'll be a stream comin' from that 'ere nozzle that'll eat into the gravel quicker than the hull lot of us, and it'll wash piles of dirt down into the catches we have made. Ter-morrer we start in right away at the real business."

It had been no easy matter to arrange their catches below the point where the water was to play upon the cliff and gravel. But Steve was a knowing fellow, and had insisted that the jet should be brought as low as possible.

"So as ter undermine the rest of the stuff," he explained. "Then it'll fall in easy."

A wooden channel was erected below the spot where the jet was to play, the width of which, great at first, narrowed steadily, while the channel itself descended at a sharp angle. Every ten feet along it bulk-heads were erected across, in wedge-shape pattern, the apex of the wedge being presented upward. Finally the channel ended in a basin, with an overflow to take the water off.

"It's down below we shall get the dust," said Tom, surveying the whole plant with no little pride. "Them iron washing troughs will soon collect it for us, and with much less diggin' than we should ha' had to do. Up here, whar the channel's steeper, and nearer the jet, we aer likely ter get nuggets. Reckon it'll pay us ter go steady. We'll play the jet first thing in the morning, till the channel and the partitions in it aer pretty full. Then we'll shut off the water, and get to at washing.

There's a trough fer each of us, and one man can do a heap, considerin' the arrangements we have made."

The whole plant was, in fact, splendidly engineered. In order to save labor, they had not only pressed the water from the stream above into their service, with the idea of making it dig by its force, and bring the gravel away from between its rocky walls; but they had so contrived matters that they could open a sluice at the bottom of the huge wooden pipe which fed the water to the jet, and could pass the contents down a narrow channel, running beside the one constructed, to catch the dirt. Suspended in this, one opposite each bulkhead, was a long wooden trough, either end faced with a plate of iron, in which Jack had bored numerous holes, small at the bottom, and getting bigger towards the top.

"They're jest like the washing troughs used by diggers," explained Tom, "and me and Steve's rocked 'em day in and day out. Yer see, the stuff one shovels into them gets broken up by the rocking, while the water carries the grit away. One pitches the big stuff out with one's hands, while the sand and the gold settles. Gee, ef after all this here preparation, we don't make a pile, why, bust me, I'll take ter scoutin' agin!"

Let the reader imagine the excitement amongst this little party on the following morning. Tom lit his pipe to show his coolness and his utter disregard of results, and clambered to the top of the cliff. But it was not the same cool Tom who had commanded the movements of the band when attacked by Indians. His hand was trembling as he manoeuvred the sluice gate above, while his anxiety to see the water shoot from the jet was that of a little boy.

"Gee-whiz! Did you ever!" he exclaimed as the water spurted from the jet, and, hitting the face of the gravel, began to dig a path into it. "Ef that ain't better than diggin'! Though it has cost a sight of labor ter get it all ready. Look how the dirt comes down. Reckon it won't be long afore we have ter pipe farther along, so as ter follow the grit."

That afternoon, when the bulkheads and the channel in which they were placed were crammed with fallen gravel, the sluice at the bottom of the wooden pipe was opened, and the spurt of water from the jet ceased. Then the various individuals of the party set to work with their shovels, and, each selecting one of the troughs, threw the stuff which had been washed down into it, and rocked vigorously, while the stream played through the holes at the head of the trough, washed the dirt, and trickled out at the farther end. The most exciting time of all had arrived. Each one of the party wondered if, when he had labored for a while, and had at length cleared away the débris, he would find the bottom of his trough filled with common sand, or whether amidst the yellow particles there would be others, gleaming bright in the sunshine, the gold for which he labored and on which he had set his heart.

"Gee! Come here, boys!"

It was a shout from Tom that broke the trying silence that had fallen upon Jack and his comrades at their several troughs, and at the sound they flung down their spades, or ceased rocking the cradles, and hastened to the side of the hunter. Tom's face was flushed a brick red, which extended under his sunburn down over neck and chest and arms. The pipe gripped between his teeth was wabbling and trembling strangely, while this habitually cool man was actually shivering with excitement.

"Boys," he said in a thin voice, as if he were dazed, "didn't we come here fer gold, ter find somethin' to pay us fer all them weeks of travel, fer fightin' with the Injuns, and fer all the labor we've put in here? Say, ain't thet it?"

"Guess so," answered Steve laconically, while the others nodded, some briskly, with a smile of expectation, others with a grin; for Tom's obvious excitement was catching, while others again jerked their heads in a curiously spasmodic manner, and stood looking at the scout awkwardly, as if ashamed to show too much interest, and yet disclosing by the brightness of their eyes the undoubted fact that they were eager for his news.

"Wall!" asked Jacob. "You've struck it, eh? I ain't had time ter look into my little lot, but others may have done."

"And I ain't had time to get searchin' in amongst all the stuff that's left in my cradle," cried Tom, blurting the words out rapidly. "But yer kin see whar I am. Top of the lot of yer, jest whar all the heavy stuff is sure ter lie. Yer see, the fall is thet sharp that light stuff and grit gets washed over the catch jest here. Only big stones and suchlike gets caught. Wall, aer that a stone?"

His face was all wrinkled with smiles, as Tom flung out the hand which up till that moment he had held behind him. In the open palm a dirty, discoloured object of irregular shape was lying, and at a rough guess it was nearly as large as a cricket ball. The scout turned it over, and then moved his hand in a half-circle, bringing the object beneath the eyes of each one of his partners in turn. Then Steve stepped forward, and, taking the mass, as if it were actually only a common stone, threw it up some few inches into the air, and repeated the process. Passing it to his mouth he then tried his teeth on the surface, and finally, with a quick stride, stepping to the side of the little stream which delivered water to the washing troughs, he dipped the object in it, rinsed it thoroughly, and then brought it into the strong sunlight again. And now it had changed its character. The mass was no longer soiled and discoloured. It was of a dull, golden colour, deeply scored here and there where the shape was most irregular, and displaying a perfectly smooth, rounded surface in other parts. In the very centre of this rounded part, emerging half an inch from the golden mass was a splinter of flint, firmly embedded in the metal.

"Boys," said Steve coolly, though the little scout's eyes were strangely bright, "I 'low as this aer the evenin' when we kin have a picnic in the camp. We ha' worked hard, and travelled far, and it aer gold we've come fer. Wall, thar it is. Thar's a nugget, ef ever I saw one, and it's tidy sartin it ain't the only one as we shall drop upon. Ef thet's the case, me and you, mates, will have somethin' ter take back with us ter repay us fer all the labor. Thet bein' so, it aer clear thet it aer Jacob's duty ter bring out thet bottle of spirits ter-night. Abe, too, might get to pretty soon and cook us a meal that'll lick anythin' we've touched this many a month."

10

STRIKING IT RICH

BY JAMES OLIVER CURWOOD

In this excerpt from author James Oliver Curwood's fine novel The Gold Hunters, *we get a vivid portrait of what it was like to finally reach the grounds where the prospectors expected to find gold.*

Slowly out of that mysterious gloom there grew a shape before Rod's eyes. At first it was only a shadow, then it might have been a rock, and then the gulp in his throat leaped out in a shout when he saw that Wabigoon's sharp eyes had in truth discovered the old cabin of the map. For what else could it be? What else but the wilderness home of the adventurers whose skeletons they had found, Peter Plante and Henri Langlois, and John Ball, the man whom these two had murdered?

Rod's joyous voice was like the touch of fire to Wabi's enthusiasm and in a moment the oppressive silence of their journey down the chasm was broken by the wild cheers which the young gold seekers sent echoing between the mountains. Grimacing and chuckling in his own curious way, Mukoki was already slipping along the edge of the rock, seeking some break by which he might reach the lower chasm. They were on the point of turning to the ascent of the mountain, along which they would have to go until they found such a break, when the old pathfinder directed the attention of his companions to the white top of a dead cedar stub projecting over the edge of the precipice.

"Go down that, mebby," he suggested, shrugging his shoulders to suggest that the experiment might be a dangerous one.

Rod looked over. The top of the stub was within easy reach, and the whole tree was entirely free of bark or limbs, a fact which in his present excitement did not strike him as especially unusual. Swinging his rifle strap over his shoulders he reached out, caught the slender apex

of the stub, and before the others could offer a word of encouragement or warning was sliding down the wall of the rock into the chasm.
Wabi was close behind him, and not waiting for Mukoki's descent the
two boys hurried toward the cabin. Half-way to it Wabi stopped.

"This isn't fair. We've got to wait for Muky."

They looked back. Mukoki was not following. The old warrior was
upon his knees at the base of the dead tree, as though he was searching
for something among the rocks at its foot. Then he rose slowly, and
rubbed his hands along the stub as high as he could reach. When he
saw that Rod and Wabi were observing him he quickly came toward
them, and Wabigoon, who was quick to notice any change in him, was
confident that he had made a discovery of some kind.

"What have you found, Muky?"

"No so ver' much. Funny tree," grunted the Indian.

"Smooth as a fireman's brass pole," added Rod, seeing no significance in Mukoki's words. "Listen!"

He stopped so suddenly that Wabigoon bumped into him from
behind.

"Did you hear that?"

"No."

For a few moments the three huddled close together in watchful
silence. Mukoki was behind the boys or they would have seen that his
rifle was ready to spring to his shoulder and that his black eyes were
snapping with something not aroused by curiosity alone. The cabin
was not more than twenty paces away. It was old, so old that Rod
wondered how it had withstood the heavy storms of the last winter.
A growth of saplings had found root in its rotting roof and the logs of
which it was built were in the last stage of decay. There was no window, and where the door had once been there had grown a tree a foot
in diameter, almost closing the narrow aperture through which the

mysterious inhabitants had passed years before. A dozen paces, five paces from this door, and Mukoki's hand reached out and laid itself gently upon Wabi's shoulder. Rod saw the movement and stopped. A strange look had come into the old Indian's face, an expression in which there was incredulity and astonishment, as if he believed and yet doubted what his eyes beheld. Mutely he pointed to the tree growing before the door, and to the reddish, crumbling rot into which the logs had been turned by the passing of generations.

"Red pine," he said at last. "That cabin more'n' twent' t'ous'nd year old!"

There was an awesome ring in his voice. Rod understood, and clutched Wabi's arm. In an instant he thought of the other old cabin, in which they had found the skeletons. They had repaired that cabin and had passed the winter in it, and they knew that it had been built half a century or more before. But this cabin was beyond repair. To Rod it seemed as though centuries of time instead of decades had been at work on its timbers. Following close after Wabi he thrust his head through the door. Deep gloom shut out their vision. But as they looked, steadily inuring their eyes to the darkness within, the walls of the old cabin took form, and they saw that everywhere was vacancy. There was no ancient table, as in the other cabin they had discovered at the head of the first chasm, there were no signs of the life that had once existed, not even the remnants of a chair or a stool. The cabin was bare.

Foot by foot the two boys went around its walls. Mukoki took but a single glance inside and disappeared. Once alone he snapped down the safety of his rifle. Quickly, as if he feared interruption, he hurried around the old cabin, his eyes close to the earth. When Rod and Wabi returned to the door he was at the edge of the fall, crouching low among the rocks like an animal seeking a trail. Wabi pulled his companion back.

"Look!"

The old warrior rose, suddenly erect, and turned toward them, but the boys were hidden in the gloom. Then he hurried to the dead stub beside the chasm wall. Again he reached far up, rubbing his hand along its surface.

"I'm going to have a look at that tree!" whispered Wabi. "Something is puzzling Mukoki. Are you coming?"

He hurried across the rock-strewn opening, but Rod hung back. He could not understand his companions. For weeks and months they had planned to find this third waterfall. Visions of a great treasure had been constantly before their eyes, and now that they were here, with the gold perhaps under their very feet, both Mukoki and Wabigoon were more interested in a dead stub than in their search for it! His own heart was almost bursting with excitement. The very air which he breathed in the old cabin set his blood leaping with anticipation. Here those earlier adventurers had lived half a century or more ago. In it the life-blood of the murdered John Ball might have ebbed away. In this cabin the men whose skeletons he had found had slept, and planned, and measured their gold. And the gold! It was that and not the stub that interested Roderick Drew! Where was the lost treasure? Surely the old cabin must hold some clue for them, it would at least tell them more than the limbless white corpse of a tree!

From the door he looked back into the dank gloom, straining his eyes to see, and then glanced across the opening. Wabi had reached the stub, and both he and Mukoki were on their knees beside it. Probably they have found the marks of a lynx or a bear, thought Rod. A dozen paces away something else caught his eyes, a fallen red pine, dry and heavy with pitch, and in less than a minute he had gone to it and was back with a torch. Breathlessly he touched the tiny flame of a match to the stick. For a moment the pitch sputtered and hissed, then flared into light, and Rod held the burning wood above his head.

The young gold seeker's first look about him was disappointing. Nothing but the bare walls met his eyes. Then, in the farthest corner, he observed something that in the dancing torch-light was darker than the logs themselves, and he moved toward it. It was a tiny shelf, not more than a foot long, and upon it was a small tin box, black and rust-eaten by the passing of ages. With trembling fingers Rod took it in his hand. It was very light, probably empty. In it he might find the dust of John Ball's last tobacco. Then, suddenly, as he thought of this, he stopped in his search and a muffled exclamation of surprise fell from him. In the glow of the torch he looked at the tin box. It was crumbling with age and he might easily have crushed it in his hand—and yet it was still a tin box! If this box had remained, why had not other things? Where were the pans and kettles, the pail and frying-pan, knives, cups and other articles which John Ball and the two Frenchmen must at one time have possessed in this cabin?

He returned to the door. Mukoki and Wabigoon were still at the dead stub. Even the flare of light in the old cabin had not attracted them. Tossing his torch away Rod tore off the top of the tin box. Something fell at his feet, and as he reached for it he saw that it was a little roll of paper, almost as discolored as the rust-eaten box itself. As gently as Mukoki had unrolled the precious birchbark map a few months before he smoothed out the paper. The edges of it broke and crumbled under his fingers, but the inner side of the roll was still quite white. Mukoki and Wabigoon, looking back, saw him suddenly turn toward them with a shrill cry on his lips, and the next instant he was racing in their direction, shouting wildly at every step.

"The gold!" he shrieked. "The gold! Hurrah!"

He was almost sobbing in his excitement when he stopped between them, holding out the bit of paper.

"I found it in the cabin—in a tin box! See, it's John Ball's writing—the writing that was on the old map! I found it—in a tin box—"

Wabi seized the paper. His own breath came more quickly when he saw what was upon it. There were a few lines of writing, dim but still legible, and a number of figures. Across the top of the paper was written:

"Account of John Ball, Henri Langlois, and Peter Plante for month ending June thirtieth, 1859."

Below these lines was the following:

Plante's work: nuggets, 7 pounds, nine ounces; dust, 1 pound, 3 ounces.

Langlois' work: nuggets, 9 pounds, 13 ounces; dust, none.

Ball's work: nuggets, 6 pounds, 4 ounces; dust, 2 pounds, 3 ounces.

Total, 27 pounds.

Plante's share, 6 pounds, 12 ounces.

Langlois' share, 6 pounds, 12 ounces.

Ball's share, 13 pounds, 8 ounces.

Division made.

Softly Wabigoon read the words aloud. When he finished his eyes met Rod's, Mukoki was still crouching at the foot of the stub, staring at the two boys in silence, as if stupefied by what he had just heard.

"This doesn't leave a doubt," said Wabi at last. "We've struck the right place!"

"The gold is somewhere—very near—"

Rod could not master the tremble in his voice. As though hoping to see the yellow treasure heaped in a pile before his eyes he turned to the waterfall, to the gloomy walls of the chasm, and finally extended an arm to where the spring torrent, leaping over the edge of the chasm above, beat itself into frothing rage among the rocks between the two mountains.

"It's there!"

"In the stream?"

"Yes. Where else near this cabin would they have found pure nuggets of gold? Surely not in rock! And gold-dust is always in the sands of streams. It's there—without a doubt!"

Both Indians went with him to the edge of the water.

"The creek widens here until it is very shallow," said Wabi. "I don't believe that it is more than four feet deep out there in the middle. What do you say—" He paused as he saw Mukoki slip back to the dead stub again, then went on, "What do you say to making a trip to the canoe after grub for our dinner, and the pans?"

The first flash of enthusiasm that had filled Wabigoon on reading the paper discovered by Rod was quickly passing away, and the white youth could not but notice the change which came over both Mukoki and his young friend when they stood once more beside the smooth white stub that reached up to the floor of the chasm above. He controlled his own enthusiasm enough to inspect more closely the dead tree which had affected them so strangely. The discovery he made fairly startled him. The surface of the stub was not only smooth and free of limbs, but was polished until it shone with the reflecting luster of a waxed pillar! For a moment he forgot the paper which he held in his hand, forgot the old cabin, and the nearness of gold. In blank wonder he stared at Mukoki, and the old Indian shrugged his shoulders.

"Ver' nice an' smooth!"

"Ver' dam' smooth!" emphasized Wabi, without a suggestion of humor in his voice.

"What does it mean?" asked Rod.

"It means," continued Wabigoon, "that this old stub has for a good many years been used by something as a sort of stairway in and out of this chasm! Now if it were a bear, there would be claw marks. If it were a lynx, the surface of the stub would be cut into shreds. Any kind of animal would have left his mark behind, and no animal would have put this polish on it!"

"Then what in the world—"

Rod did not finish. Mukoki lifted his shoulders to a level with his chin, and Wabi whistled as he looked straight at him.

"Not a hard guess, eh?"

"You mean—"

"That it's a man! Only the arms and legs of a man going up and down that stub hundreds and thousands of times could have worn it so smooth! Now, can you guess who that man is?"

In a flash the answer shot into Rod's brain. He understood now why this old stub had drawn his companions away from their search for gold, and he felt the flush of excitement go out of his own cheeks, and an involuntary thrill pass up his back.

"The mad hunter!"

Wabi nodded. Mukoki grunted and rubbed his hands.

"Gold in bullet come from here!" said the old pathfinder. "Bad dog man ver' swift on trail. We hurry get canoe—cut down tree!"

"That's more than you've said in the last half-hour, and it's a good idea!" exclaimed Wabi. "Let's get our stuff down here and chop this stub into firewood! When he comes back and finds his ladder gone he'll give a screech or two, I'll wager, and then it will be our chance to do something with him. Here goes!"

He started to climb the stub, and a minute or two later stood safely on the rock above.

"Slippery as a greased pole!" he called down. "Bet you can't make it, Rod!"

But Rod did, after a tremendous effort that left him breathless and gasping by the time Wabi stretched out a helping hand to him. Mukoki came up more easily. Taking only their revolvers with them the three hurried to the birch bark, and in a single load brought their possessions to the rock. By means of ropes the packs and other contents of the canoe, and finally the canoe itself, were lowered into the chasm, and while the others looked on Mukoki seized the ax and chopped down the stub.

"There!" he grunted, as a last blow sent the tree crashing among the rocks. "Too high for heem jump!"

"But a mighty good place for him to shoot from," said Wabi, looking up. "We'd better camp out of range."

"Not until we know what we've struck," cried Rod, unstrapping a pan from one of the packs. "Boys, the first thing to do is to wash out a little of that river-bed!"

He started for the creek, with Wabi close behind him bearing a second pan. Mukoki looked after them and chuckled softly to himself as he began making preparations for dinner. Choosing a point where the current had swept up a small bar of pebbles and sand Wabi and

Rod both set to work. The white youth had never before panned gold, but he had been told how it was done, and there now shot through him that strange, thrilling excitement which enthralls the treasure hunter when he believes that at last he has struck pay dirt. Scooping up a quantity of the gravel and sand he filled his pan with water, then moved it quickly back and forth, every few moments splashing some of the "wash" or muddy water, over the side. Thus, filling and refilling his pan with fresh water, he excitedly went through the process of "washing" everything but solid substance out of it.

With each fresh dip into the stream the water in the pan became clearer, and within fifteen minutes the three or four double handfuls of sand and gravel with which he began work dwindled down to one. Scarcely breathing in his eagerness he watched for the yellow gleam of gold. Once a glitter among the pebbles drew a low cry from him, but when with the point of his knife he found it to be only mica he was glad that Wabi had not heard him. The young Indian was squatting upon the sand, with his pan turned toward a gleam of the sun that shot faintly down into the chasm. Without raising his head he called to Rod.

"Found anything?"

"No. Have you?"

"No—yes—but I don't think it's gold."

"What does it look like?"

"It gleams yellow but is as hard as steel."

"Mica!" said Rod.

Neither of the boys looked up during the conversation. With the point of his hunting-knife Rod still searched in the bottom of his pan, turning over the pebbles and raking the gravelly sand with a painstaking care that would have made a veteran gold seeker laugh. Some minutes had passed when Wabi spoke again.

"I say, Rod, that's a funny-looking thing I found! If it wasn't so hard I'd swear it was gold? Want to see it?"

"It's mica," repeated Rod, as another gleam of "fool's gold" in his own pan caught his eyes. "The stream is full of it!"

"Never saw mica in chunks before," mumbled Wabi, bending low over his pan.

"Chunks!" cried Rod, straightening as if some one had run a pin into his back. "How big is it?"

"Big as a pea—a big pea!"

The words were no sooner out of the young Indian's mouth than Roderick was upon his feet and running to his companion.

"Mica doesn't come in chunks! Where—"

He bent over Wabi's pan. In the very middle of it lay a suspiciously yellow pebble, worn round and smooth by the water, and when Rod took it in his fingers he gave a low whistle of mock astonishment as he gazed down into Wabigoon's face.

"Wabi, I'm ashamed of you!" he said, trying hard to choke back the quiver in his voice. "Mica doesn't come in round chunks like this. Mica isn't heavy. And this is *both*!"

From the cedars beyond the old cabin came Mukoki's whooping signal that dinner was ready.

11

STORM AND STRESS

BY W. H. P. JARVIS

In his book The Great Gold Rush, *author W. H. P. Jarvis produced one of the most detailed looks at the fortunes and misfortunes of gold-seekers in the Yukon. The quest there was not an easy one, and, as you will see in this excerpt, from the very beginning prospectors were hearing reports that their venture was doomed. (Editor's note: this story has been edited from the original.)*

It was five o'clock on the morrow before the party was up, and six o'clock before, breakfast cooked and eaten, John and Hugh were on the road to the summit. They were to travel the twenty miles there, and return with one thousand pounds of supplies.

The glow of the sun was already upon the mountains when they set out.

"Say! it's going to be a hot day, and it's going to thaw some. It'll make hauling easy, but our feet will be pretty wet; good thing we've got some dry socks and rubbers in our outfit at the summit. Another thing is, we're going to meet a whole lot of fellows on the trail the way we're going to-day; and, what's worse, we'll get more of them coming back."

Sure enough, after they left Log Cabin, they could see the toilers coming, winding in a snake-like procession among the hills.

Hugh had prophesied correctly. By eleven o'clock they were in their shirt-sleeves. The dazzling whiteness of the snow, reflected from all sides, made the use of smoke-glasses necessary; but the perspiration, dimming the glass, troubled their sight. The end of John's nose became painful; his cheeks burned. It reminded him of the after-effects of his first sunny spring day on the water in England.

They met and passed scores of teams, and still more were pouring over the summit when they arrived there at one o'clock. It was half-past two before they had their feet encased in German socks and rubber shoes, and their load ready again for the trail.

"We can't make home before dark, but we should be able to make Log Cabin by seven, after which the trail will be clear, and we should arrive by ten. This trail will be mighty good going after it starts to freeze, which it will do, soon as the sun goes down."

At four o'clock they were three miles on the trail. There was already frost in the air.

Ere another half-hour had passed Hugh felt his cheek smitten by a gust of wind, laden with particles of ice.

"I thought so!" he exclaimed; "these last few days have shown too large a pay streak of spring to last. We're in for trouble. It will be down on us in half an hour. All we can do is to keep on as we are going, steadily. I guess we shall make Log Cabin, but not with this load. The soft snow makes a thousand pounds too much for the dogs. Look!" He pointed to a miniature cyclone coming along the trail, drinking up the ice particles as it whirled. It struck them sharply as a gust of wind.

The first contact of the storm was cold and cutting; then the wind veered, and down came the snow. The sleigh was soon too heavy.

"The only thing is to cache the sleigh and turn the dogs loose; the chances are we won't be able to keep the trail in this storm; and if we do come out alive, we won't be able to find the sleigh if we abandon it far from the trail."

"Do you think the storm will be very bad?"

"It's bad now, ain't it? How long will it be before there is eighteen inches of snow on this trail? For a time we can keep it by feeling it hard under us; but we are liable to get off it—and once lost, there is no finding it again. Mind, the wind is blowing from the right, half to the rear. Here's a tree; I've noticed this lone spruce before, and we can find it again. Let us stand the sleigh up against it, and turn the dogs loose."

So to the tree dogs and men struggled; the dogs were unhitched, harness was piled on top of the load. Then, with a great effort, the men managed to up-end the load against the tree.

Hugh called Dude to him, and pulled an old envelope out of his pocket, on which he scratched: "Cached sleigh on north side of trail by spruce tree, five miles from the summit.—Hugh Spencer." This he tied to a handkerchief, and that to Dude's collar.

"It's no harm letting George know where the grub is, for if we don't find camp again, Dude will."

The dogs went, Dude leading, and were soon lost to sight.

Down the trail the two men strode. The snow was six inches deep already, the wind piling it upon the trail. The weather did not feel cold; in fact, both were comfortably warm. For an hour they plodded along. Occasionally one would plunge into the soft snow and scramble back on to the beaten trail. Conversation was not much indulged in.

The light began to fail, yet they stumbled along. There was nothing they could recognize in the boulders and cliffs that loomed around them in a deathly monotony.

For half an hour darkness was upon them, when Hugh remarked that Log Cabin could not be far away. Immediately following his remark they plunged into soft snow. The trail seemed to have come to an end; but this could not be so. They retraced their steps and regained firm footing. They felt cautiously around with their feet, but could find the underlying snow hard only in the direction whence they came.

"I guess we're off the trail, and have walked along a bank where the wind has packed the old snow good and hard. Looks to me as if we was lost."

"Don't give up," said John.

"Give up! I ain't giving up; but we're lost. I won't give up as long as I can wiggle."

"What had we better do?"

"Keep moving! If you don't, you freeze!" Spencer's voice was low and serious as he said, "Keep the wind on your right side; and if you've got any last will and testament to make, scratch it on a piece of paper and leave it in your pocket before your hands get numb, or your mind weak. We're up against it hard! We will stay together, of course; but should we get separated, don't move too fast, or you will tire yourself out and go to sleep in the snow. Don't let sleep take hold of you, or you're dead! Just keep moving fast enough to keep warm, or, at least, from freezing; go down hill rather than up; and don't fall over a cliff. Have you ever been up against a life-and-death proposition? If not, you are pretty near one now."

They proceeded on their uncertain journey, but were soon floundering in soft snow. They kept on. It was easy enough to say "keep going down-hill," but, so far as John was concerned, he seemed to be walking up-hill all the time. They frequently exchanged shouts, and so remained together.

For hours they plodded on, the snowfall growing less, but the cold greater.

John began to act, to call, mechanically. His mind in that desolate trampling was transported to happier places. He thought of his Alice Peel. She was probably, he mused, thinking of him also. Did her mind ever picture such experiences as he was now realizing? She would possibly read in the newspapers of the great rush of gold-seekers over those terrible mountains and through the stormy passes. If he should die in that storm, and months afterwards she heard of his demise? . . . The thought drifted along to several loose ends. He must not sleep, or he would die; and it was his duty to live; but—oh! to sleep! . . . His father, and the old school, the church services! How much he would like to hear the old organ and the choir! . . . It had been the family wish that he should take Holy Orders, and he had refused the vocation, feeling it not his. Had he done right? He believed yes. . . . He might be about to meet his Creator. What might his record be? . . . His mind went back to an occasion in Australia, when he had been lost in the Bush, and had wandered for days without water, till some blacks found him. He remembered, before going into unconsciousness with his back against a rock, that a vulture was watching him. He had taken a piece of stone, and, pretending it was a pistol, had pointed it at the bird . . .

John Berwick's mind was picturing sand and heat, while above him roared the Arctic storm.

How cold it was getting, and the wind was beginning to blow! The parka did not sufficiently protect his face.

Hugh shouted out that they were crossing a lake, and there might be a camp along its edge. They came in due course to the other side of the lake, with the cliff so steep they could not climb it. They followed the shore to the right, facing the storm. They crossed another lake, and still another. The air had grown intensely cold; the wind was higher, and ever there came that terrible inclination to lie down and sleep.

After they had passed over the last little lake Hugh shouted to John that they were surely now far from the proper trail, as he could recollect no such water near Bennett. Lake Lindeman was four miles long.

The wind was rising, and the increasing cold told that it came from the north. Hugh began now really to doubt whether they would live through the storm.

Soon afterwards fine ice crystals impinged against their faces. Great swirls of wind fell upon them. This new severe onslaught of nature aroused John, who called to his comrade. He had suddenly realized how very, very close they were to death.

"The snow is going—it's easier walking," he said suddenly.

They closed together, and struggled along abreast. They were too nearly dead to notice that the going was good. Suddenly John fell into the soft snow, and Hugh, exerting his worn powers, dragged him back.

"The trail, the trail," gasped John, with his face close to Hugh's.

"Trail! we ain't been on any trail for hours."

"Feel with your feet!"

Hugh stopped to feel with his feet two runner tracks of horse sled. Hope came to them, made a great call to their resources. Meanwhile their tired hearts and very weary bodies endured the bombardment of the snow-laden wind, which seemed to penetrate them, taking the heat of life from their vitals!

They came to another lake. How the wind cut! The snow, driven over the surface of the ice, gave a hard, grinding noise. Would ever they come to the end of that pitiless journey!

Bang! They stumbled against a sleigh standing in the middle of the road. Hugh kicked at it; the singletree rattled; he recognized the sound. He gave a desperate shout; another and another.

Then, at last, the promise of relief and of life came to them. They smelt smoke. Just for a second!—that creosotic odour was to them as sweetest perfume. It meant life, warmth, comfort, human companionship.

The figure of a man with a lantern loomed up before them, and a deep voice asked, "What's the matter?"

"We're lost," said John.

"No, you're not; you're right here on Crater Lake, just over the summit of the Chilkoot."

"Thank God!" said Hugh.

"We're the police; come inside." They staggered into a tent warmed by a tin stove, on which was a pot of coffee. The man quickly produced cups, and gave them to drink.

John Berwick just fell on a pile of wood, stacked near the stove, and fell asleep. Now that the great struggle against the elements, which force of personality rather than strength of limbs had carried him through, was over, he collapsed.

When the policeman returned with bread and meat for them, he found Hugh removing his friend's shoes, and brushing the snow from his legs.

"Let him sleep," said Hugh.

~~~~~~

After two hours of solid sleep, the blanket was lifted from the exhausted gold-seekers, and they were shaken back into life.

"Get up and eat, you need it."

Still aching in every bone the two poor fellows staggered to their feet.

A dim light was penetrating the canvas, as they looked about them. Underneath was ice—the frozen surface of Crater Lake—on which were spread piles of blankets, the beds of the police.

Notwithstanding the fire, the air of the tent was chill and frosty, and the canvas flapped in the wind. The walls of the tent were dark, showing the level of the snow around them. The presence of this snow, no doubt, explained how the tent had withstood the fury of the gale.

The policeman led the way to the cook tent, where they were given bacon and slap-jacks.

"Can't make bread here, and don't get it very often from Dyea, and we're just out now," apologized the policeman who acted as cook.

While they were eating ravenously, the officer in command of the post called to see them and inquired if they were any the worse for their experiences.

"Hardly salubrious, the climate, eh?" he said, after they had answered his particular questions. "On several occasions we have had the tents blown down, and frequently the men had to sit up all night holding the poles to prevent a catastrophe. I must say our fellows have shown great grit under most trying circumstances. You see we are on a civil campaign here, and there is not the excitement of fighting to keep the men up."

With that the officer left the tent. A policeman glanced after him and muttered, "Civil campaign! Hear the old man talk! We're holding down the blooming Passes for the Queen! That's what we're doing. We could live in comfort at Lindeman, with all the wood we want for cabins and to burn."

"Where do you get your wood?"

"Down the trail—when we get any at all. They send a horse up from Lindeman. The last few days the trail has been pretty good, and some teams have been hauling from there to here; but we got only one load—which won't last us through the storm, if it holds much longer."

"Do you collect much duty here?"

"Well—rather! The old man just dumps the money he takes in a leather sack, and the other day he had thirty-five thousand dollars in it; but he hasn't got that much now. He sent one of the fellows down to Skagway with it. It was rather risky, for all the hard cases travelling the Passes got to know the sack; and there was a good deal of risk of the fellow getting shot; but he went through the whole gang and got on the boat at Dyea, and crossed to Skagway."

"The man had pluck!"

"Yes; but human nature in many ways is alike in both red-skin and white men, and the police have learned to do these sort of things. Down on the plains in the old days, when the natives were mean, it was often the case that one or two policemen would ride into a reservation, arrest a man, and take him away with hundreds of armed Indians yelling around them. The Indians thought the police were crazy, and it is against their religion to kill a crazy man. I guess if Soapy recognized the sack he thought it was a job of some kind."

"Do as many men come over this Pass as over the White Pass?"

"More! The Chilkoot is the poor man's Pass. Most of the fellows who come over here haul their own stuff, and pack it over the summit, or hire the Siwashes to put it to the summit, and haul from here themselves. They get it up here, and then, when they get a fine day, run it through to Lindeman or Bennett, where they build their boats. An outfit is putting in an aerial tram: that is, a cable from the foot of the big hill to the top."

"This summit is too steep for horses?"

"Oh, yes. It's as much as an ordinary man wants to climb it light, and it's much worse with a pack on your back, though a Siwash staggered up the other day with a cask of tar weighing three hundred and fifty pounds. The sad part of it was that then he could not get his five cents, a pound for his work!—at least he came to one of our fellows, who told him to hide the barrel in the snow and not show the owner where it was, till he got his money. Wait till you see the hill! It is one of the most remarkable sights, I fancy, ever seen in the world's history: thousands of men toiling in line up nine hundred feet of almost perpendicular ascent—for what?—to be given a chance of drowning themselves in the Yukon, or of dying of disease in the Dawson country!"

The time came for the evening meal; but the storm still raged outside and the weather remained cold. It would be hard to conceive more miserable surroundings! The heat given out by the stove was scarcely felt six feet away, and the icy floor, snow walls, and flimsy roof sapped the body's heat. Darkness came, and bed-time. Two policemen offered to share their bed with the guests, so that the strangers had somewhere to lay their heads.

It appeared to John that he had just fallen to sleep when he was awakened by the sentry calling to all hands to dress, as water was overflowing the ice and coming into the tent. So up all hands got, hastily dressing in the frosty atmosphere. By the uncertain light of a few flickering candles water was to be seen entering the tent; and what was the best move was a matter of discussion, till one policeman suggested that sleighs be hauled into the tent, and the beds built on them. This was done, but not before a good portion of the bedding had become wet.

Let any one who desires a picture of the hardships which policemen and civilians went through in those dreadful Passes imagine the poor fellows living in tents, with water six inches deep within, a storm surging without—and the thermometer many degrees below freezing-point! It was three more days ere the wind ceased to blow, and for those three days the police and their guests existed under distressing conditions. At the end of the three days milder weather came; but the water still remained on the ice, so that it was plain the camp must be moved. Preparations were being made to do this when John and Hugh bade their kindly hosts good-bye.

12

THE POCKET HUNTER

BY MARY AUSTIN

Even though the lure of gold was a beacon to multitudes of prospectors, its siren call was often answered by bold men who went into the wilderness alone. The spirit and fate of these intrepid prospectors was clearly presented in Jack London's "All Gold Canyon," the first story in this book. Here, writer Mary Austin presents another portrait of the gold-seekers who were determined to strike it rich on their own, without partners or help of any kind. (Editor's note: this story has been edited from the original.)

I remember very well when I first met him. Walking in the evening glow, I sniffed the unmistakable odor of burning sage. It is a smell that carries far and indicates usually the nearness of a camp, but on the level mesa nothing taller showed than sage. Over the tops of it, beginning to dusk under a young white moon, trailed a wavering ghost of smoke, and at the end of it I came upon the Pocket Hunter making a dry camp in the friendly scrub. He sat tailor-wise in the sand, with his coffee-pot on the coals, his supper ready to hand in the frying-pan, and himself in a mood for talk. His pack burros in hobbles strayed off to hunt for a wetter mouthful than the sage afforded, and gave him no concern.

We came upon him often after that, threading the windy passes, or by water-holes in the desert hills, and got to know much of his way of life. He was a small, bowed man, with a face and manner and speech of no character at all, as if he had that faculty of small hunted things of taking on the protective color of his surroundings. His clothes were of no fashion that I could remember, except that they bore liberal markings of pot black, and he had a curious fashion of going about with his mouth open, which gave him a vacant look until you came near enough to perceive him busy about an endless hummed, word-less tune. He traveled far and took a long time to it, but the simplicity of his kitchen arrangements was elemental. A pot for beans, a coffee-pot, a frying-pan, a tin to mix bread in—he fed the burros in this when there was need—with these he had been half round our western world and back. He explained to me very early in our acquaintance what was good to take to the hills for food: nothing sticky, for that "dirtied the pots"; nothing with "juice" to it, for that would not pack to advan-tage; and nothing likely to ferment. He used no gun, but he would set snares by the water-holes for quail and doves, and in the trout country he carried a line. Burros he kept, one or two according to his pack, for this chief excellence, that they would eat potato parings and firewood. He had owned a horse in the foothill country, but when he came to the desert with no forage but mesquite, he found himself under the necessity of picking the beans from the briers, a labor that drove him to the use of pack animals to whom thorns were a relish.

I suppose no man becomes a pocket hunter by first intention. He must be born with the faculty, and along comes the occasion, like the tap on the test tube that induces crystallization. My friend had been several things of no moment until he struck a thousand-dollar pocket in the Lee District and came into his vocation. A pocket, you must know, is a small body of rich ore occurring by itself, or in a vein of poorer stuff. Nearly every mineral ledge contains such, if only one has the luck to hit upon them without too much labor. The sensible thing for a man to do who has found a good pocket is to buy himself into business and keep away from the hills. The logical thing is to set out looking for another one. My friend the Pocket Hunter had been look-ing twenty years. His working outfit was a shovel, a pick, a gold pan which he kept cleaner than his plate, and a pocket magnifier. When he came to a watercourse he would pan out the gravel of its bed for "colors," and under the glass determine if they had come from far or near, and so spying he would work up the stream until he found where the drift of the gold-bearing outcrop fanned out into the creek; then up the side of the cañon till he came to the proper vein. I think he said the best indication of small pockets was an iron stain, but I could never get the run of miner's talk enough to feel instructed for pocket hunting. He had another method in the waterless hills, where he would work in and out of blind gullies and all windings of the manifold strata that appeared not to have cooled since they had been heaved up. His itinerary began with the east slope of the Sierras of the Snows, where that range swings across to meet the coast hills, and all up that slope to the Truckee River country, where the long cold forbade his progress north. Then he worked back down one or another of the nearly parallel ranges that lie out desertward, and so down to the sink of the Mojave River, burrowing to oblivion in the sand,—a big mysterious land, a lonely, inhospitable land, beautiful, terrible. But he came to no harm in it; the land tolerated him as it might a gopher or a badger. Of all its inhabitants it has the least concern for man.

There are many strange sorts of humans bred in a mining country, each sort despising the queernesses of the other, but of them all I found the Pocket Hunter most acceptable for his clean, companionable talk. There was more color to his reminiscences than the faded sandy old miners "kyoteing," that is, tunneling like a coyote (kyote in the vernacular) in the core of a lonesome hill. Such a one has found, perhaps, a body of tolerable ore in a poor lead,—remember that I can never be depended on to get the terms right,—and followed it into the heart of country rock to no profit, hoping, burrowing, and hoping. These men go harmlessly mad in time, believing themselves just behind the wall of fortune—most likable and simple men, for whom it is well to do any kindly thing that occurs to you except lend them money. I have known "grub stakers" too, those persuasive sinners to whom you make allowances of flour and pork and coffee in consideration of the ledges they are about to find; but none of these proved so much worth while as the Pocket Hunter. He wanted nothing of you and maintained a cheerful preference for his own way of life. It was an excellent way if you had the constitution for it. The Pocket Hunter had gotten to that point where he knew no bad weather, and all places were equally happy so long as they were out of doors. I do not know just how long it takes to become saturated with the elements so that one takes no account of them. Myself can never get past the glow and exhilaration of a storm, the wrestle of long dust-heavy winds, the play of live thunder on the rocks, nor past the keen fret of fatigue when the storm outlasts physical endurance. But prospectors and Indians get a kind of a weather shell that remains on the body until death.

The Pocket Hunter had seen destruction by the violence of nature and the violence of men, and felt himself in the grip of an All-wisdom that killed men or spared them as seemed for their good; but of death by sickness he knew nothing except that he believed he should never suffer it. He had been in Grape-vine Canon the year of storms that changed the whole front of the mountain. All day he had come down under the wing of the storm, hoping to win past it, but finding it traveling with him until night. It kept on after that, he supposed, a steady downpour, but could not with certainty say, being securely deep in sleep. But the weather instinct does not sleep. In the night the heavens behind the hill dissolved in rain, and the roar of the storm was borne in and mixed with his dreaming, so that it moved him, still asleep, to get up and out of the path of it. What finally woke him was the crash of pine logs as they went down before the unbridled flood, and the swirl of foam that lashed him where he clung in the tangle of scrub while the wall of water went by. It went on against the cabin of Bill

Gerry and laid Bill stripped and broken on a sand bar at the mouth of the Grape-vine, seven miles away. There, when the sun was up and the wrath of the rain spent, the Pocket Hunter found and buried him; but he never laid his own escape at any door but the unintelligible favor of the Powers.

The journeyings of the Pocket Hunter led him often into that mysterious country beyond Hot Creek where a hidden force works mischief, mole-like, under the crust of the earth. Whatever agency is at work in that neighborhood, and it is popularly supposed to be the devil, it changes means and direction without time or season. It creeps up whole hillsides with insidious heat, unguessed until one notes the pine woods dying at the top, and having scorched out a good block of timber returns to steam and spout in caked, forgotten crevices of years before. It will break up sometimes blue-hot and bubbling, in the midst of a clear creek, or make a sucking, scalding quicksand at the ford. These outbreaks had the kind of morbid interest for the Pocket Hunter that a house of unsavory reputation has in a respectable neighborhood, but I always found the accounts he brought me more interesting than his explanations, which were compounded of fag ends of miner's talk and superstition. He was a perfect gossip of the woods, this Pocket Hunter, and when I could get him away from "leads" and "strikes" and "contacts," full of fascinating small talk about the ebb and flood of creeks, the pinon crop on Black Mountain, and the wolves of Mesquite Valley. I suppose he never knew how much he depended for the necessary sense of home and companionship on the beasts and trees, meeting and finding them in their wonted places,—the bear that used to come down Pine Creek in the spring, pawing out trout from the shelters of sod banks, the juniper at Lone Tree Spring, and the quail at Paddy Jack's.

There is a place on Waban, south of White Mountain, where flat, wind-tilted cedars make low tents and coves of shade and shelter, where the wild sheep winter in the snow. Woodcutters and prospectors had brought me word of that, but the Pocket Hunter was accessory to the fact. About the opening of winter, when one looks for sudden big storms, he had attempted a crossing by the nearest path, beginning the ascent at noon. It grew cold, the snow came on thick and blinding, and wiped out the trail in a white smudge; the storm drift blew in and cut off landmarks, the early dark obscured the rising drifts. According to the Pocket Hunter's account, he knew where he was, but couldn't exactly say. Three days before he had been in the west arm of Death Valley on a short water allowance, ankle-deep in shifty sand; now he was on the rise of Waban, knee-deep in sodden snow, and in both cases he did the only allowable thing—he walked on. That is the only thing to do in a snowstorm in any case. It might have been the creature instinct, which in his way of life had room to grow, that led him to the cedar shelter; at any rate he found it about four hours after dark, and heard the heavy breathing of the flock. He said that if he thought at all at this juncture he must have thought that he had stumbled on a storm-belated shepherd with his silly sheep; but in fact he took no note of anything but the warmth of packed fleeces, and snuggled in between them dead with sleep. If the flock stirred in the night he stirred drowsily to keep close and let the storm go by. That was all until morning woke him shining on a white world. Then the very soul of him shook to see the wild sheep of God stand up about him, nodding their great horns beneath the cedar roof, looking out on the wonder of the snow. They had moved a little away from him with the coming of the light, but paid him no more heed. The light broadened and the white pavilions of the snow swam in the heavenly blueness of the sea from which they rose. The cloud drift scattered and broke billowing in the canons. The leader stamped lightly on the litter to put the flock in motion, suddenly they took the drifts in those long light leaps that are nearest to flight, down and away on the slopes of Waban. Think of that to happen to a Pocket Hunter! But though he had fallen on many a wished-for hap, he was curiously inapt at getting the truth about beasts in general. He believed in the venom of toads, and charms for snake bites, and—for this I could never forgive him—had all the miner's prejudices against my friend the coyote. Thief, sneak, and son of a thief were the friendliest words he had for this little gray dog of the wilderness.

Of course with so much seeking he came occasionally upon pockets of more or less value, otherwise he could not have kept up his way of life; but he had as much luck in missing great ledges as in finding small ones. He had been all over the Tonopah country, and brought away float without happening upon anything that gave promise of what that district was to become in a few years. He claimed to have chipped bits off the very outcrop of the California Rand, without finding it worth while to bring away, but none of these things put him out of countenance.

It was once in roving weather, when we found him shifting pack on a steep trail, that I observed certain of his belongings done up in green canvas bags, the veritable "green bag" of English novels. It seemed so incongruous a reminder in this untenanted West that I dropped down beside the trail overlooking the vast dim valley, to hear about the green canvas. He had gotten it, he said, in London years before, and that was the first I had known of his having been abroad. It was after one of his "big strikes" that he had made the Grand Tour, and had brought nothing away from it but the green canvas bags, which he conceived would fit his needs, and an ambition. This last was nothing less than to strike it rich and set himself up among the eminently bourgeois of London.

It seemed that the situation of the wealthy English middle class, with just enough gentility above to aspire to, and sufficient smaller fry to bully and patronize, appealed to his imagination, though of course he did not put it so crudely as that.

It was no news to me then, two or three years after, to learn that he had taken ten thousand dollars from an abandoned claim, just the sort of luck to have pleased him, and gone to London to spend it. The land seemed not to miss him any more than it had minded him, but I missed him and could not forget the trick of expecting him in least likely situations. Therefore it was with a pricking sense of the familiar that I followed a twilight trail of smoke, a year or two later, to the swale of a dripping spring, and came upon a man by the fire with a coffee-pot and frying-pan. I was not surprised to find it was the Pocket Hunter. No man can be stronger than his destiny.

13

THE NORTH WIND'S MALICE

BY REX BEACH

Novelist Rex Beach (1877–1949) was a writer whose prose skills were often turned to tales of the north. The Klondike Gold Rush was a prime subject for Beach's considerable storytelling talents, as this tale shows with vigor.

It had snowed during the night, but toward morning it had grown cold; now the sled-runners complained and the load dragged heavily. Folsom, who had been heaving at the handle-bars all the way up the Dexter Creek hill, halted his dogs at the crest and dropped upon the sled, only too glad of a breathing spell. His forehead was wet with sweat; when it began to freeze in his eyebrows he removed his mittens and wiped away the drops, then watched them congeal upon his fingers. Yes, it was all of thirty below, and a bad morning to hit the trail, but—Folsom's face set itself—better thirty below in the open than the frigid atmosphere of an unhappy home.

Harkness, who had led the way up the hill, plodded onward for a time before discovering that his companion had paused; then, through the ring of hoar frost around his parka hood, he called back:

"I'll hike down to the road-house and warm up."

Folsom made no answer, he did not even turn his head. Taciturnity was becoming a habit with him, and already he was beginning to dislike his new partner. For that matter he disliked everybody this morning.

Below him lay the level tundra, merging indistinguishably with the white anchor-ice of Behring Sea; beyond that a long black streak of open water, underscoring the sky as if to emphasize the significance of that empty horizon, a horizon which for many months would remain unsmudged by smoke. To Folsom it seemed that the distant stretch of dark water was like a prison wall, barring the outside world from him and the other fools who had elected to stay "inside."

Fools? Yes; they were all fools!

Folsom was a "sour-dough." He had seen the pranks that Alaskan winters play with men and women, he had watched the alteration in minds and morals made by the Arctic isolation, and he had considered himself proof against the malice that rides the north wind—the mischief that comes with the winter nights. He had dared to put faith in his perfect happiness, thinking himself different from other men and Lois superior to other wives, wherefore he now called himself a fool!

Sprawled beside the shore, five miles away, was Nome, its ugliness of corrugated iron, rough boards, and tar paper somewhat softened by the distance. From the jumble of roofs he picked out one and centered his attention upon it. It was his roof—or had been. He wondered, with a sudden flare of wrathful indignation, if Lois would remember that fact during his absence. But he banished this evil thought. Lois had pride, there was nothing common about her; he could not believe that she would affront the proprieties. It was to spare that very pride of hers, even more than his own, that he had undertaken this adventure to the Kobuk; and now, as he looked back upon Nome, he told himself that he was acting handsomely in totally eliminating himself, thus allowing her time and freedom in which to learn her heart. He hoped that before his return she would have chosen between him and the other man.

It was too cold to remain idle long. Folsom's damp body began to chill, so he spoke to his team and once more heaved upon the handle-bars.

Leaving the crest of the ridge behind, the dogs began to run; they soon brought up in a tangle at the road-house door. When Harkness did not appear in answer to his name Folsom entered, to find his trail-mate at the bar, glass in hand.

"Put that down!" Folsom ordered, sharply.

Harkness did precisely that, then he turned, wiping his lips with the back of his hand. He was a small, fox-faced man; with a grin he invited the new-comer to "have one."

"Don't you know better than to drink on a day like this?" the latter demanded.

"Don't worry about me. I was raised on 'hootch,'" said Harkness.

"It's bad medicine."

"Bah! I'll travel further drunk than"—Harkness measured his critic with an insolent eye—"than some folks sober." He commenced to warm himself at the stove, whereupon the other cried, impatiently:

"Come along. We can't stop at every cabin."

But Harkness was in no hurry, he consumed considerable time. When he finally followed Folsom out into the air the latter, being in a peculiarly irritable mood, warned him in a voice which shook with anger:

"We're going to start with an understanding. If you take another drink during the daytime I'll leave you flat."

"Rats! How you aim to get to the Kobuk without me?" asked Harkness.

"I'll manage somehow."

The smaller man shot a startled glance at the speaker, then his insolence vanished. "All right, old top," he said, easily. "But don't cut off your nose to spite your face. Remember, I promised if you'd stick to me you'd wear gold-beaded moccasins." He set off at a trot, with the dogs following.

This fellow Harkness had come with the first snow into Nome, bearing news of a strike on the Kobuk, and despite his braggadocio he had made rather a good impression. That luck which favors fools and fakers had guided him straight to Folsom. He had appeared at a psychological moment in the latter's affairs, two disastrous seasons having almost broken Folsom and rendered him eager to grasp at anything which promised quick returns; moreover, the latter had just had a serious quarrel with his wife. Harkness had offered a half interest in his Kobuk claims for a grubstake and a working partner, and, smarting under the unaccustomed sting of domestic infelicity, the other had accepted, feeling sure in his own mind that Lois would not let him leave her when the time came to go. But the time had come, and Lois had offered no objection. She had acted strangely, to be sure, but she had made no effort to dissuade him. It seemed as if the proposal to separate for the winter had offended rather than frightened her. Well, that was the way with women; there was no pleasing them; when you tried to do the decent thing by them they pretended to misunderstand your motives. If you paid them the compliment of utter confidence they abused it on the pretext that you didn't love them; if you allowed your jealousy to show, they were offended at your lack of trust.

So ran the husband's thoughts. He hoped that six months of widowhood would teach Lois her own mind, but it hurt to hit the trail with nothing more stimulating than a listless kiss and a chill request to write when convenient. Now that he was on his way he began to think of the pranks played by malicious nature during the long, dark nights, and to wonder if he had acted wisely in teaming up with this footless adventurer. He remembered the malice that rides the winter winds, the mischief that comes to Arctic widows, and he grew apprehensive.

The travelers put up that night at the Tin Road-house, a comfortless shack sheathed with flattened kerosene cans, and Folsom's irritation at his new partner increased, for Harkness was loud, boastful, and blatantly egotistical, with the egotism that accompanies dense ignorance.

The weather held cold, the snow remained as dry as sand, so they made slow progress, and the husband had ample time to meditate upon his wrongs, but the more he considered them the less acutely they smarted him and the gentler became his thoughts of Lois. The solitudes were healing his hurt, the open air was cooling his anger.

At Kougarok City, a miserable huddle of cottonwood cabins, Harkness escaped his partner's watchful eye and got drunk. Folsom found the fellow clinging to the bar and entertaining a crowd of loafers with his absurd boastings. In a white fury he seized the wretch, dragged him from the room, and flung him into his bunk, then stood guard over him most of the night.

It was during the quieter hours when the place rumbled to snores that Folsom yielded to his desire to write his wife, a desire which had been growing steadily. He was disgusted with Harkness, disappointed with the whole Kobuk enterprise, and in a peculiarly softened mood, therefore, he wrote with no attempt to conceal his yearning, homesick tenderness.

But when he read the letter in the morning it struck him as weak and sentimental, just the sort of letter he would regret having written if it should transpire that Lois did not altogether share his feelings.

So he tore it up.

Those were the days of faint trails and poor accommodations; as yet the road to the Arctic was little traveled and imperfectly known, so Harkness acted as guide. He had bragged that he knew every inch of the country, but he soon proved that his ideas of distance were vague and faulty—a serious shortcoming in a land with no food, no shelter, and no firewood except green willows in the gulch-bottoms. Folsom began to fear that the fellow's sense of direction was equally bad, and taxed him with it, but Harkness scoffed at the idea.

Leaving the last road-house behind them, they came into a hilly section of great white domes, high hog-backs, and ramifying creeks, each one exactly like its neighbor; two days' travel through this, according to Harkness, should have brought them to the Imnachuck, where there was food and shelter again. But when they pitched camp for the second night Folsom felt compelled to remind his partner that they were behind their schedule, and that this was the last of their grub.

"Are you sure you're going right?" he inquired.

"Sure? Of course I'm sure. D'you think I'm lost?"

Folsom fed some twisted willow-tops into the sheet-iron stove. "I wouldn't recommend you as a pathfinder," said he. "You said we'd sleep out one night. This is two, and to-morrow we'll walk hungry."

"Well, don't blame me!" challenged the other. "I'm going slow on your account."

Now nothing could have galled Folsom more than a reflection upon his ability to travel. His lips whitened, he was upon the point of speaking his mind, but managed to check himself in time. Harkness's personality rasped him to the raw, and he had for days struggled against an utterly absurd but insistent desire to seize the little coxcomb by the throat and squeeze the arrogance out of him as juice is squeezed out of a lemon. There is flesh for which one's fingers itch.

"I notice you're ready to camp when I am," the larger man muttered. "Understand, this is no nice place to be without grub, for it's liable to storm any hour, and storms last at this season."

"Now don't get cold feet." Harkness could be maddeningly patronizing when he chose. "Leave it to me. I'll take you a short cut, and we'll eat lunch in a cabin to-morrow noon."

But noon of the next day found Harkness still plodding up the river with the dogs close at his heels. The hills to the northward were growing higher, and Folsom's general knowledge of direction told him that they were in danger of going too far.

"I think the Imnachuck is over there," said he.

Harkness hesitated, then he nodded: "Right-o! It's just over that low saddle." He indicated a sweeping hillside ahead, and a half-mile further on he left the creek and began to climb. This was heavy work for the dogs, and mid-afternoon came before the partners had gained the summit only to discover that they were not upon a saddleback after all, but upon the edge of a vast rolling tableland from which a fanlike system of creeks radiated. In all directions was a desolate waste of barren peaks.

Folsom saw that the sky ahead was thick and dark, as if a storm impended, and realizing only too well the results of the slightest error in judgment he called to Harkness. But the latter pretended not to hear, and took advantage of the dogs' fatigue to hurry out of earshot. It was some time before the team overhauled him.

"Do you know where you are?" Folsom inquired.

"Certainly." Harkness studied the panorama spread before him. "That blue gulch yonder is the Imnachuck." He pointed to a valley perhaps four miles away.

A fine snow began to sift downward. The mountain peaks to the northward became obscured as by thin smoke, the afternoon shortened with alarming swiftness. Night, up here with a blizzard brewing, was unthinkable, so after a while the driver called another halt.

"Something informs me that you're completely lost," he said, mildly.

"Who, me? There she is." Harkness flung out a directing hand once more.

Folsom hesitated, battling with his leaping desires, and upon that momentary hesitation hinged results out of all proportions to the gravity of the situation—issues destined to change the deepest channels of his life. Folsom hesitated, then he yielded to his impulse, and the luxury of yielding made him drunk. He walked around the sled, removing his mittens with his teeth as he went. Without a word he seized his companion by the throat and throttled him until his eyes protruded and his face grew black and bloated. He relaxed his stiff fingers finally, then he shook the fellow back to consciousness.

"Just as I thought," he cried, harshly. "That's not the gulch you pointed out before. You're lost and you won't admit it."

Harkness pawed the air and fought for his breath. There was abject terror in his eyes. He reeled away, but saw there was no safety in flight.

"Own up!" Folsom commanded.

"You—said this was the way," the pathfinder whimpered. "You made me—turn off—" Folsom uttered a growl and advanced a step, whereupon his victim gurgled: "D-don't touch me! That's the Imnachuck, so help me God! I'm—I'm almost sure it is."

"Almost!" The speaker stooped for his mittens and shook the snow out of them; he was still struggling to control himself. "Look here, Mr. Know-It-All, I've never been here before, and you have; somewhere in your thick skull there must be some faint remembrance of the country. You got us into this fix, and I'm going to give you one more chance to get us out of it. Don't try to think with your head, let your feet think for you, and maybe they'll carry you to the right gulch. If they don't—" Folsom scanned the brooding heavens and his lips compressed. "We're in for a storm and—we'll never weather it. Take one look while there's light to see by, then turn your feet loose and pray that they lead you right, for if they don't, by God, I'll cut you loose!"

It soon proved that memory lay neither in Harkness's head nor in his feet; when he had veered aimlessly about for half an hour, evidently fearing to commit himself to a definite course, and when the wind came whooping down, rolling a twilight smother ahead of it, Folsom turned his dogs into the nearest depression and urged them to a run. The grade increased, soon brittle willow-tops brushed against the speeding sled: this brush grew higher as the two men, blinded now by the gale, stumbled onward behind the team. They emerged from the gulch into a wider valley, after a while, and a mile further on the dogs burst through a grove of cottonwoods and fetched up before a lighted cabin window.

Harkness pulled back his parka hood and cried, boastfully: "What did I tell you? I knew where I was all the time." Then he went in, leaving his partner to unhitch the team and care for it.

Friendships ripen and enmities deepen quickly on the trail, seeds of discord sprout and flourish in the cold. Folsom's burst of temper had served to inflame a mutual dislike, and as he and Harkness journeyed northward that dislike deepened into something akin to hatred, for the men shared the same bed, drank from the same pot, endured the same exasperations. Nothing except their hope of mutual profit held them together. In our careless search for cause and effect we are accustomed to attribute important issues to important happenings, amazing consequences to amazing deeds; as a matter of fact it is the trivial action, the little thing, the thing unnoticed and forgotten which bends our pathways and makes or breaks us.

Harkness was a hare-brained, irresponsible person, incapable of steadiness in thought or action, too weak to cherish actual hatred, too changeable to nurse a lasting grudge. It is with such frail instruments that prankish fate delights to work, and, although he never suspected it, the luxury of yielding to that sudden gust of passion cost Folsom dear.

Arrived finally at the Kobuk the miner examined the properties covered by his option, and impressed by the optimism of the men who had made the gold discovery he paid Harkness the price agreed upon. The deal completed, he sent the fellow back to Candle Creek, the nearest post, for supplies. Folsom's mood had altogether changed by now, so, strangling his last doubt of Lois, he wrote her as he had written at Kougarok City, and intrusted the letter to his associate.

Harkness, promptly upon his arrival at Candle, got drunk. He stayed drunk for three days, and it was not until he was well started on his way back to the Kobuk that he discovered Folsom's letter still in his pocket.

Now, to repeat, the man was not malicious, neither was he bad, but as he debated whether he should back-track there came to him the memory of his humiliation on the Imnachuck divide.

So! His brains were in his feet, eh? Folsom had strangled him until he kicked, when, all the time, they had been on the right trail. Harkness felt a flash of rage, like the flare of loose gunpowder, and in the heat of it he tore the letter to atoms. It was a womanish, spiteful thing to do, and he regretted it, but later when he greeted the husband he lied circumstantially and declared he had given the missive into the hands of the mail-carrier on the very hour of his departure. By this time, doubtless, it was nearly to Nome. Soon thereafter Harkness forgot all about the incident.

Folsom was a fast worker. He hired men and cross-cut the most promising claim. Bed-rock was shallow, and he soon proved it to be barren, so he went on to the next property. When he had prospected this claim with no better results than before he wrote his wife confessing doubts of the district and voicing the fear that his winter's work would be wasted. Again he let his pen run as it would; the letter he gave to a neighbor who was leaving for Candle Creek in the morning.

Folsom's neighbor was a famous "musher," a seasoned, self-reliant man, thoroughly accustomed to all the hazards of winter travel, but ten miles from his destination he crossed an inch-deep overflow which rendered the soles of his muk-luks slippery, and ten yards further on, where the wind had laid the glare-ice bare, he lost his footing. He fell and wrenched his ankle and came hobbling into Candle half an hour after the monthly mail for Nome had left.

Three weeks later Folsom wrote his wife for the third time, and again a month after that. All three letters joined company in Candle Creek; for meanwhile the mail-man's lead dog had been killed in a fight with a big malamute at Lane's Landing, causing its owner to miss a trip. Now dog-fights are common; by no logic could one attribute weighty results to the loss of a sixty-pound leader, but in this instance it so happened that the mail-carrier's schedule suffered so that his contract was canceled.

Meanwhile a lonely woman waited anxiously in Nome, and as the result of a stranger's spite, a wet muk-luk, and a vicious malamute her anxiety turned to bitterness and distrust.

It is never difficult to forward mail in the north, for every "musher" is a postman. When news came to Candle Creek that the Government service had been discontinued the storekeeper, one end of whose bar served as post-office, sacked his accumulated letters and intrusted them to some friends who were traveling southward on the morrow. The trader was a canny man, but he loved to gamble, so when his friends offered to bet him that they could lower the record from Candle to Nome he went out into the night, sniffed the air and studied the stars, then laid them a hundred dollars that they could not.

Excited to recklessness by this wager the volunteer mail-men cut down their load. They left their stove and tent and grub-box behind, planning to make a road-house every night except during the long jump from the Imnachuck to Crooked River. They argued that it was worth a hundred dollars to sleep once under the open sky.

The fruits of that sporting enterprise were bitter; the trader won his bet, but he never cashed it in. Somewhere out on the high barrens a storm swooped down upon the travelers. To one who has never faced an Arctic hurricane it seems incredible that strong men have died within call of cozy cabins or have frozen with the lashings of their sleds but half untied. Yet it is true. The sudden awful cold, the shouting wind, the boiling, blinding, suffocating rush of snow; the sweaty clothes that harden into jointless armor; the stiff mittens and the clumsy hands inside—these tell a tale to those who know.

The two mail-carriers managed to get into their sleeping-bags, but the gale, instead of drifting them over with a protective mantle of snow, scoured the mountain-side bare to the brittle reindeer moss, and they began to freeze where they lay. Some twenty hours they stood it, then they rose and plunged ahead of the hurricane like bewildered cattle. The strongest man gave up first and lay down, babbling of things to eat. His companion buried him, still alive, and broke down the surrounding willow-tops for a landmark, then he staggered on. By some miracle of good luck, or as a result of some unsuspected power of resistance, he finally came raving into the Crooked River Road-house. When the wind subsided they hurried him to Nome, but he was frightfully maimed and as a result of his amputations he lay gabbling until long after the spring break-up.

Folsom did not write again. In fact, when no word came from Lois, he bitterly regretted the letters he had written. He heard indirectly from her; new-comers from Nome told him that she was well, but that was all. It was enough. He did not wish to learn more.

Spring found him with barely enough money to pay his way back. He was blue, bitter, disheartened, but despite the certainty that his wife had forsaken him he still cherished a flickering hope of a reconciliation. Strangely enough he considered no scheme of vengeance upon the other man, for he was sane and healthy, and he loved Lois too well to spoil her attempt at happiness.

It so happened that the Arctic ice opened up later this spring than for many seasons; therefore the short summer was well under way before the first steam-schooner anchored off the Kobuk. Folsom turned his back upon the wreck of his high hopes, his mind solely engaged with the problem of how to meet Lois and ascertain the truth without undue embarrassment to her and humiliation to himself. The prospect of seeing her, of touching her, of hearing her voice, affected him painfully. He could neither eat nor sleep on the way to Nome, but paced the deck in restless indecision. He had come to consider himself wholly to blame for their misunderstanding, and he wished only for a chance to win back her love, with no questions asked and no favors granted.

When there were less than fifty miles to go the steamer broke her shaft. There was no particular reason why that shaft should break, but break it did, and for eighteen hours—eighteen eternities to Folsom— the ship lay crippled while its engine-room crew labored manfully.

Folsom had been so long in the solitudes that Nome looked like a big city when he finally saw it. There were several ships in the road-stead, and one of them was just leaving as the Kobuk boat came to anchor. She made a splendid sight as she gathered way.

The returning miner went ashore in the first dory and as he stepped out upon the sand a friend greeted him:

"Hello there, old settler! Where you been all winter?"

"I've been to the Kobuk," Folsom told him.

"Kobuk? I hear she's a bum."

"'Bum' is right. Maybe she'll do to dredge some day."

"Too bad you missed the *Oregon*; there she goes now." The man pointed seaward.

"Too bad?"

"Sure! Don't you know? Why, Miz Folsom went out on her!"

Folsom halted; after a momentary pause he repeated, vaguely, "Went out?"

"Exactly. Didn't you know she was going?"

"Oh yes—of course! The *Oregon!*" Folsom stared at the fading plume of black smoke; there was a curious brightness in his eyes, his face was white beneath its tan. "She sailed on the *Oregon* and I missed her, by an hour! That broken shaft—" He began to laugh, and turning his back upon the sea he plodded heavily through the sand toward the main street.

Folsom found no word from his wife, his house was empty; but he learned that "the man" had also gone to the States, and he drew his own conclusions. Since Lois had ordered her life as she saw fit there was nothing to do but wait and endure—doubtless the divorce would come in time. Nevertheless, he could not think of that broken shaft without raving.

Being penniless he looked for work, and his first job came from a small Jewish merchant, named Guth, who offered him a hundred dollars to do the assessment work on a tundra claim. For twenty days Folsom picked holes through frozen muck, wondering why a thrifty person like Guth would pay good money to hold such unpromising property as this.

The claim was in sight of Nome, and as Folsom finished his last day's labor he heard bells ringing and whistles blowing and discovered that the town was ablaze. He hurried in to find that an entire block in the business center of the city had been destroyed and with it Guth's little store, including all its contents. He found the man in tears.

"What a misfortune!" wailed the merchant. "Ruined, absolutely— and by a match! It started in my store—my little girl, you understand?

And now, all gone!" He tore his beard and the tears rolled down his cheeks.

The little man's grief was affecting, and so Folsom inquired more gently than he intended, "I'm sorry, of course, but how about my money for the Lulu assessment?"

"Money? There's your money!" Guth pointed sadly into the smoldering ruins. "Go find it—you're welcome to anything I have left. Gott! What a country! How can a man get ahead, with no insurance?"

Folsom laughed mirthlessly. His hard luck was becoming amusing and he wondered how long it would last. He had counted on that hundred dollars to get away from Nome, hoping to shake misfortune from his heels, but a match in the hands of a child, like that broken propeller shaft, had worked havoc with his plans. Well, it was useless to cry.

To the despairing Hebrew he said: "Don't lose your grip, old man. Buck up and take another start. You have your wife and your little girl, at least, and you're the sort who makes good."

"You think so?" Guth looked up, grateful for the first word of encouragement he had heard.

"It's a cinch! Only don't lose your courage."

"I—I'll do what's right by you, Mr. Folsom," declared the other. "I'll deed you a half interest in the Lulu."

But Folsom shook his head. "I don't want it. There's nothing there except moss and muck and salmon berries, and it's a mile to bed-rock. No, you're welcome to my share; maybe you can sell the claim for enough to make a new start or to buy grub for the wife and the kid. I'll look for another job."

For a month or more the lonesome husband "stevedored," wrestling freight on the lighters, then he disappeared. He left secretly, in the night, for by now he had grown fanciful and he dared to hope that he could dodge his Nemesis. He turned up in Fairbanks, a thousand miles away, and straightway lost himself in the hills.

He had not covered his tracks, however, for bad luck followed him.

Now no man starves in Alaska, for there is always work for the able-bodied; but whatever Folsom turned his hand to failed, and by and by his courage went. He had been a man of consequence in Nome; he had made money and he had handled other men, therefore his sense of failure was the bitterer.

Meanwhile, somewhere in him there remained the ghost of his faith in Lois, the faintly flickering hope that some day they would come together again. It lay dormant in him, like an irreligious man's unacknowledged faith in God and a hereafter, but it, too, vanished when he read in a Seattle newspaper, already three months old, the announcement of his wife's divorce. He flinched when he read that it had been won on the grounds of desertion, and thereafter he shunned newspapers.

Spring found him broke, as usual. He had become bad company and men avoided him. It amused him grimly to learn that a new strike had been made in Nome, the biggest discovery in the camp's history, and to realize that he had fled just in time to miss the opportunity of profiting by it. He heard talk of a prehistoric sea-beach line, a streak of golden sands which paralleled the shore and lay hidden below the tundra mud. News came of overnight fortunes, of friends grown prosperous and mighty. Embittered anew, Folsom turned again to the wilderness, and he did not reappear until the summer was over. He came to town resolved to stay only long enough to buy bacon and beans, but he had lost his pocket calendar and arrived on a Sunday, when the stores were closed.

Even so little a thing as the loss of that calendar loomed big in the light of later events, for in walking the streets he encountered a friend but just arrived from the Behring coast.

The man recognized him, despite his beard and his threadbare mackinaws and they had a drink together.

"I s'pose you heard about that Third Beach Line?" the new-comer inquired. Folsom nodded. "Well, they've opened it up for miles, and it's just a boulevard of solid gold. 'Cap' Carter's into it big, and so are the O'Brien boys and Old Man Hendricks. They're lousy with pay."

"I did the work on a tundra claim," said Folsom; "the Lulu—"

"The Lulu!" Folsom's friend stared at him. "Haven't you heard about the Lulu? My God! Where you been, anyhow? Why, the Lulu's a mint! Guth is a millionaire and he made it all without turning a finger."

Folsom's grip on the bar-rail tightened until his knuckles were white.

"I'm telling you right, old man; he's the luckiest Jew in the country. He let a lay to McCarthy and Olson, and they took out six hundred thousand dollars, after Christmas."

"Guth offered me a half interest in the Lulu when his store burned and—I turned it down. He's never paid me for that assessment work."

The Nomeite was speechless with amazement. "The son-of-a-gun!" he said, finally. "Well, you can collect now. Say! That's what he meant when he told me he wanted to see you. Guth was down to the boat when I left, and he says: 'If you see Folsom up river tell him to come back. I got something for him.' Those were his very words. That little man aims to pay you a rotten hundred so you won't sue him for an interest. By Gorry, I wouldn't take it! I'd go back and make him do the right thing. I'd sue him. I'd bust him in the nose! A half interest—in the Lulu! My God!" The speaker gulped his drink hastily.

After consideration, Folsom said: "He'll do the right thing. Guth isn't a bad sort."

"No. But trust him to get his."

"I wouldn't ask him to do more than pay his debt. You see I refused his offer."

"What of that? I'd give it a try, anyhow, and see if he wouldn't settle. There's lots of lawyers would take your case. But say, that's the toughest tough-luck story I ever heard. You've sure got a jinx on you."

"I'm going back, but I won't sue Guth. I'm sick of Alaska; it has licked me. I'm going out to God's country."

Folsom indeed acknowledged himself beaten. The narrow margin by which he had missed reward for his work and his hardships bred in him such hatred for Alaska that he abruptly changed his plans. He had no heart, perversity had killed his courage. It exasperated him beyond all measure to recall what little things his luck had hinged upon, what straws had turned his feet. A moment of pique with Lois, a broken piece of steel, a match, a momentary whim when Guth offered him payment. It was well that he did not know what part had been played by his quarrel with Harkness, that wet muk-luk, that vicious lead dog, and the storekeeper's wager.

Folsom carried cord-wood to pay for a deck passage down river. He discovered en route that Guth had really tried to get in touch with him, and in fact appeared greatly concerned over his failure to do so, for at Tanana he received another message, and again at St. Michaels. He was grimly amused at the little Jew's craftiness, yet it sorely offended him to think that any one should consider him such a welcher. He had no intention of causing trouble, for he knew he had no legal claim against the fellow, and he doubted if he possessed even a moral right to share in the Lulu's riches. To play upon the Hebrew's fears, therefore, savored of extortion. Nevertheless, he was in no agreeable frame of mind when he arrived at his destination and inquired for Guth.

The new-made millionaire was in his office; Folsom walked in unannounced. He had expected his arrival to create a scene, and he was not disappointed. But Guth's actions were strange, they left the new arrival dazed, for the little man fell upon him with what appeared to be exuberant manifestations of joy.

"Mr. Folsom!" he cried. "You have come! You got my letters, eh? Well, I wrote you everywhere, but I was in despair, for I thought you must be dead. Nobody knew what had become of you."

"I got your message in Fairbanks."

"You heard about the Lulu, eh? Gott! She's a dandy."

"Yes. I can hardly believe it. So, you're rich. Well, I congratulate you, and now I can use that hundred."

Guth chuckled. "Ha! You will have your joke, eh? But the Lulu is no joke. Come, we will go to the bank; I want them to tell you how much she has yielded. You'll blame me for leasing her, but how was I to know what she was?"

"I—Why should I blame—" Folsom stared at the speaker. "It's none of my business what the Lulu has yielded. In fact, I'll sleep better if I don't know."

Little Guth paused and his mouth opened. After a moment he inquired, curiously: "Don't you understand?" There was another pause, then he said, quietly, "I'm a man of my word."

Folsom suddenly saw black, the room began to spin, he passed his hand across his eyes. "Wait! Let's get this straight," he whispered.

"It is all very simple," Guth told him. "We are equal partners in the Lulu—we have been, ever since the day my store burned. It was a little thing you said to me then, but the way you said it, the fact that you didn't blame me, gave me new heart. Did you think I'd renig?" When

Folsom found no answer the other nodded slowly. "I see. You probably said, 'That Guth will do me up if he can.' But I am an honest man, too, like you."

Folsom turned to the wall and hid his face in the crook of his arm, but with his other hand he groped for that of the Hebrew.

The story of the Lulu is history now; in all the north that mine is famous, for it made half a dozen fortunes. In a daze, half doubting the reality of things, Folsom watched a golden stream pour into his lap. All that winter and the next summer the Lulu yielded wondrously, but one of the partners was not happy, his thoughts being ever of the woman who had left him. Prosperity gave him courage, however, and when he discovered that Lois had not remarried he determined to press his luck as a gambler should.

When the second season's sluicing was over and the ground had frozen he went outside.

The day after he sailed Lois arrived in Nome, on the last boat. She was older, graver; she had heard of the Lulu, but it was not that which had brought her back. She had returned in spite of the Lulu to solve an aching mystery and to learn the why of things. Her husband's riches—she still considered him her husband—merely made the task more trying.

Advised that Folsom had passed almost within hailing distance of her, she pressed her lips together and took up her problem of living. The prospect of another lonely Alaskan winter frightened her, and yet because of the Lulu she could not return by the ship she had come on. Now that Folsom was a Croesus she could not follow him too closely—he might misunderstand. After all, she reflected, it mattered little to her where she lived.

Guth called at her cabin, but she managed to avoid seeing him, and somehow continued to avoid a meeting.

Late in December some travelers from Candle Creek, while breaking a short cut to the head of Crooked River, came upon an abandoned sled and its impedimenta. Snow and rain and summer sun had bleached its wood, its runners were red streaks of rust, its rawhide lashings had been eaten off, but snugly rolled inside the tarpaulin was a sack of mail. This mail the travelers brought in with them, and the Nome newspapers, in commenting upon the find, reprinted the story of that tragic fight for life in the Arctic hurricane, now almost forgotten.

Folsom's three letters reached their destination on Christmas Day. They were stained and yellow and blurred in places, for they were three years old, but the woman read them with eyes wide and wondering, and with heart-beats pounding, for it seemed that dead lips spoke to her. Ten minutes later she was standing at Guth's door, and when he let her in she behaved like one demented. She had the letters hidden in her bosom, and she would not let him see them, but she managed to make known the meaning of her coming.

"You know him," she cried, hysterically. "You made him rich. You've lived alongside of him. Tell me then, has he . . . has he . . . changed? These letters are old. Does he still care, or . . . does he hate me, as he should?"

Guth smiled; he took her shaking hands in his, his voice was gentle. "No, no! He doesn't hate you. He has never mentioned your name to me, or to any one else, so far as I know, but his money hasn't satisfied him. He is sad, and he wants you. That is what took him to the States, I'm sure."

Lois sank into a chair, her face was white, her twisting fingers strained at each other. "I can't understand. I can't make head or tail of it," she moaned. "It seems that I wronged him, but see what ruin he has made for me! Why? Why—?"

"Who can understand the 'why' of anything?" inquired the little Hebrew. "I've heard him curse the perversity of little things, and rave at what he called the 'malice of the north wind.' I didn't dare to ask him what he meant, but I knew he was thinking of the evil which had come between you two. Who was to blame, or what separated you, he never told me. Well, his bad luck has changed, and yours, too; and I'm happy. Now then, the wireless. You can talk to him. Let us go."

An hour later a crackling message was hurled into the empty Christmas sky, a message that pulsed through the voids, was relayed over ice and brine and drifted forests to a lonely, brooding man three thousand miles away.

The answer came rushing back:

"Thank God! Am starting north tomorrow. Love and a million kisses. Wait for me."

Folsom came. Neither ice nor snow, neither winter seas nor trackless wastes, could daunt him, for youth was in his heart and fire ran through his veins. North and west he came by a rimy little steamer, as fast as coal could drive her, then overland more than fifteen hundred miles. His record stands unbroken, and in villages from Katmai to the Kuskokwim the Indians tell of the tall white man with the team of fifteen huskies who raced through as if a demon were at his heels; how he bored headlong into the blizzards and braved January's fiercest rage; how his guides dropped and his dogs died in their collars. That was how Folsom came.

He was thin and brown, the marks of the frost were bitten deep into his flesh when, one evening in early March, he drove into Nome. He had covered sixty miles on the last day's run, and his team was staggering. He left the dogs in their harnesses, where they fell, and bounded through the high-banked streets to Lois's cabin.

It was growing dark, a light gleamed from her window; Folsom glimpsed her moving about inside. He paused to rip the ice from his bearded lips, then he knocked softly, three times.

As he stood there a gentle north wind fanned him. It was deadly cold, but it was fresh and clean and vastly invigorating. There was no malice in it.

At his familiar signal he heard the clatter of a dish, dropped from nerveless fingers, he heard a startled voice cry out his name, then he pressed the latch and entered, smiling.

14

LEFT OUT ON LONE STAR MOUNTAIN

BY BRET HARTE

There was little doubt that the Lone Star claim was "played out." Not dug out, worked out, washed out, but PLAYED out. For two years its five sanguine proprietors had gone through the various stages of mining enthusiasm; had prospected and planned, dug and doubted. They had borrowed money with hearty but unredeeming frankness, established a credit with unselfish abnegation of all responsibility, and had borne the disappointment of their creditors with a cheerful resignation which only the consciousness of some deep Compensating Future could give. Giving little else, however, a singular dissatisfaction obtained with the traders, and, being accompanied with a reluctance to make further advances, at last touched the gentle stoicism of the proprietors themselves. The youthful enthusiasm which had at first lifted the most ineffectual trial, the most useless essay, to the plane of actual achievement, died out, leaving them only the dull, prosaic record of half-finished ditches, purposeless shafts, untenable pits, abandoned engines, and meaningless disruptions of the soil upon the Lone Star claim, and empty flour sacks and pork barrels in the Lone Star cabin.

They had borne their poverty, if that term could be applied to a light renunciation of all superfluities in food, dress, or ornament, ameliorated by the gentle depredations already alluded to, with unassuming levity. More than that: having segregated themselves from their fellow-miners of Red Gulch, and entered upon the possession of the little manzanita-thicketed valley five miles away, the failure of their enterprise had assumed in their eyes only the vague significance of the decline and fall of a general community, and to that extent relieved them of individual responsibility. It was easier for them to admit that the Lone Star claim was "played out" than confess to a personal bankruptcy. Moreover, they still retained the sacred right of criticism of government, and rose superior in their private opinions to their own collective wisdom. Each one experienced a grateful sense of the entire responsibility of the other four in the fate of their enterprise.

On December 24, 1863, a gentle rain was still falling over the length and breadth of the Lone Star claim. It had been falling for several days, had already called a faint spring color to the wan landscape, repairing with tender touches the ravages wrought by the proprietors, or charitably covering their faults. The ragged seams in gulch and canyon lost their harsh outlines, a thin green mantle faintly clothed the torn and abraded hillside. A few weeks more, and a veil of forgetfulness would be drawn over the feeble failures of the Lone Star claim. The charming derelicts themselves, listening to the raindrops on the roof of their little cabin, gazed philosophically from the open door, and accepted the prospect as a moral discharge from their obligations. Four of the five partners were present. The Right and Left Bowers, Union Mills, and the Judge.

It is scarcely necessary to say that not one of these titles was the genuine name of its possessor. The Right and Left Bowers were two brothers; their sobriquets, a cheerful adaptation from the favorite game of euchre, expressing their relative value in the camp. The mere fact that Union Mills had at one time patched his trousers with an old flour sack legibly bearing that brand of its fabrication, was a tempting baptismal suggestion that the other partners could not forego. The Judge, a singularly inequitable Missourian, with no knowledge whatever of the law, was an inspiration of gratuitous irony.

Union Mills, who had been for some time sitting placidly on the threshold with one leg exposed to the rain, from a sheer indolent inability to change his position, finally withdrew that weather-beaten member, and stood up. The movement more or less deranged the attitudes of the other partners, and was received with cynical disfavor. It was somewhat remarkable that, although generally giving the appearance of healthy youth and perfect physical condition, they one and all simulated the decrepitude of age and invalidism, and after limping about for a few moments, settled back again upon their bunks and stools in their former positions. The Left Bower lazily replaced a bandage that he had worn around his ankle for weeks without any apparent necessity, and the Judge scrutinized with tender solicitude the faded cicatrix of a scratch upon his arm. A passive hypochondria, born of their isolation, was the last ludicrously pathetic touch to their situation.

The immediate cause of this commotion felt the necessity of an explanation.

"It would have been just as easy for you to have stayed outside with your business leg, instead of dragging it into private life in that obtrusive way," retorted the Right Bower; "but that exhaustive effort isn't going to fill the pork barrel. The grocery man at Dalton says—what's that he said?" he appealed lazily to the Judge.

"Said he reckoned the Lone Star was about played out, and he didn't want any more in his—thank you!" repeated the Judge with a mechanical effort of memory utterly devoid of personal or present interest.

"I always suspected that man, after Grimshaw begun to deal with him," said the Left Bower. "They're just mean enough to join hands against us." It was a fixed belief of the Lone Star partners that they were pursued by personal enmities.

"More than likely those new strangers over in the Fork have been paying cash and filled him up with conceit," said Union Mills, trying to dry his leg by alternately beating it or rubbing it against the cabin wall. "Once begin wrong with that kind of snipe and you drag everybody down with you."

This vague conclusion was received with dead silence. Everybody had become interested in the speaker's peculiar method of drying his leg, to the exclusion of the previous topic. A few offered criticism, no one assistance.

"Who did the grocery man say that to?" asked the Right Bower, finally returning to the question.

"The Old Man," answered the Judge.

"Of course," ejaculated the Right Bower sarcastically.

"Of course," echoed the other partners together. "That's like him. The Old Man all over!"

It did not appear exactly what was like the Old Man, or why it was like him, but generally that he alone was responsible for the grocery man's defection. It was put more concisely by Union Mills.

"That comes of letting him go there! It's just a fair provocation to any man to have the Old Man sent to him. They can't, sorter, restrain themselves at him. He's enough to spoil the credit of the Rothschilds."

"That's so," chimed in the Judge. "And look at his prospecting. Why, he was out two nights last week, all night, prospecting in the moonlight for blind leads, just out of sheer foolishness."

"It was quite enough for me," broke in the Left Bower, "when the other day, you remember when, he proposed to us white men to settle down to plain ground sluicing, making 'grub' wages just like any Chinaman. It just showed his idea of the Lone Star claim."

"Well, I never said it afore," added Union Mills, "but when that one of the Mattison boys came over here to examine the claim with an eye to purchasin', it was the Old Man that took the conceit out of him. He just as good as admitted that a lot of work had got to be done afore any pay ore could be realized. Never even asked him over to the shanty here to jine us in a friendly game; just kept him, so to speak, to himself. And naturally the Mattisons didn't see it."

A silence followed, broken only by the rain monotonously falling on the roof, and occasionally through the broad adobe chimney, where it provoked a retaliating hiss and splutter from the dying embers of the hearth. The Right Bower, with a sudden access of energy, drew the empty barrel before him, and taking a pack of well-worn cards from his pocket, began to make a "solitaire" upon the lid. The others gazed at him with languid interest.

"Makin' it for anythin'?" asked Mills.

The Right Bower nodded.

The Judge and Left Bower, who were partly lying in their respective bunks, sat up to get a better view of the game. Union Mills slowly disengaged himself from the wall and leaned over the "solitaire" player. The Right Bower turned the last card in a pause of almost thrilling suspense, and clapped it down on the lid with fateful emphasis.

"It went!" said the Judge in a voice of hushed respect. "What did you make it for?" he almost whispered.

"To know if we'd make the break we talked about and vamose the ranch. It's the FIFTH time today," continued the Right Bower in a voice of gloomy significance. "And it went agin bad cards too."

"I ain't superstitious," said the Judge, with awe and fatuity beaming from every line of his credulous face, "but it's flyin' in the face of Providence to go agin such signs as that."

"Make it again, to see if the Old Man must go," suggested the Left Bower.

The suggestion was received with favor, the three men gathering breathlessly around the player. Again the fateful cards were shuffled deliberately, placed in their mysterious combination, with the same ominous result. Yet everybody seemed to breathe more freely, as if relieved from some responsibility, the Judge accepting this manifest expression of Providence with resigned self-righteousness.

"Yes, gentlemen," resumed the Left Bower, serenely, as if a calm legal decision had just been recorded, "we must not let any foolishness or sentiment get mixed up with this thing, but look at it like business men. The only sensible move is to get up and get out of the camp."

"And the Old Man?" queried the Judge.

"The Old Man—hush! he's coming."

The doorway was darkened by a slight lissome shadow. It was the absent partner, otherwise known as "the Old Man." Need it be added that he was a BOY of nineteen, with a slight down just clothing his upper lip!

"The creek is up over the ford, and I had to 'shin' up a willow on the bank and swing myself across," he said, with a quick, frank laugh; "but all the same, boys, it's going to clear up in about an hour, you bet. It's breaking away over Bald Mountain, and there's a sun flash on a bit of snow on Lone Peak. Look! you can see it from here. It's for all the world like Noah's dove just landed on Mount Ararat. It's a good omen."

From sheer force of habit the men had momentarily brightened up at the Old Man's entrance. But the unblushing exhibition of degrading superstition shown in the last sentence recalled their just severity. They exchanged meaning glances. Union Mills uttered hopelessly to himself: "Hell's full of such omens."

Too occupied with his subject to notice this ominous reception, the Old Man continued: "I reckon I struck a fresh lead in the new grocery man at the Crossing. He says he'll let the Judge have a pair of boots on credit, but he can't send them over here; and considering that the Judge has got to try them anyway, it don't seem to be asking too much for the Judge to go over there. He says he'll give us a barrel of pork and a bag of flour if we'll give him the right of using our tail-race and clean out the lower end of it."

"It's the work of a Chinaman, and a four days' job," broke in the Left Bower.

"It took one white man only two hours to clean out a third of it," retorted the Old Man triumphantly, "for I pitched in at once with a pick he let me have on credit, and did that amount of work this morning, and told him the rest of you boys would finish it this afternoon."

A slight gesture from the Right Bower checked an angry exclamation from the Left. The Old Man did not notice either, but, knitting his smooth young brow in a paternally reflective fashion, went on: "You'll have to get a new pair of trousers, Mills, but as he doesn't keep clothing, we'll have to get some canvas and cut you out a pair. I traded off the beans he let me have for some tobacco for the Right Bower at the other shop, and got them to throw in a new pack of cards. These are about played out. We'll be wanting some brushwood for the fire; there's a heap in the hollow. Who's going to bring it in? It's the Judge's turn, isn't it? Why, what's the matter with you all?"

The restraint and evident uneasiness of his companions had at last touched him. He turned his frank young eyes upon them; they glanced helplessly at each other. Yet his first concern was for them, his first instinct paternal and protecting. He ran his eyes quickly over them; they were all there and apparently in their usual condition. "Anything wrong with the claim?" he suggested.

Without looking at him the Right Bower rose, leaned against the open door with his hands behind him and his face towards the landscape, and said, apparently to the distant prospect: "The claim's played out, the partnership's played out, and the sooner we skedaddle out of this the better. If," he added, turning to the Old Man, "if YOU want to stay, if you want to do Chinaman's work at Chinaman's wages, if you want to hang on to the charity of the traders at the Crossing, you can do it, and enjoy the prospects and the Noah's doves alone. But we're calculatin' to step out of it."

"But I haven't said I wanted to do it ALONE," protested the Old Man with a gesture of bewilderment.

"If these are your general ideas of the partnership," continued the Right Bower, clinging to the established hypothesis of the other partners for support, "it ain't ours, and the only way we can prove it is to stop the foolishness right here. We calculated to dissolve the partnership and strike out for ourselves elsewhere. You're no longer responsible for us, nor we for you. And we reckon it's the square thing to leave you the claim and the cabin, and all it contains. To prevent any trouble with the traders, we've drawn up a paper here—"

"With a bonus of fifty thousand dollars each down, and the rest to be settled on my children," interrupted the Old Man, with a half-uneasy laugh. "Of course. But—" he stopped suddenly, the blood dropped from his fresh cheek, and he again glanced quickly round the group. "I don't think—I—I quite sabe, boys," he added, with a slight tremor of voice and lip. "If it's a conundrum, ask me an easier one."

Any lingering doubt he might have had of their meaning was dispelled by the Judge. "It's about the softest thing you kin drop into, Old Man," he said confidentially; "if I hadn't promised the other boys to go with them, and if I didn't need the best medical advice in Sacramento for my lungs, I'd just enjoy staying with you."

"It gives a sorter freedom to a young fellow like you, Old Man, like goin' into the world on your own capital, that every Californian boy hasn't got," said Union Mills, patronizingly.

"Of course it's rather hard papers on us, you know, givin' up everything, so to speak; but it's for your good, and we ain't goin' back on you," said the Left Bower, "are we, boys?"

The color had returned to the Old Man's face a little more quickly and freely than usual. He picked up the hat he had cast down, put it on carefully over his brown curls, drew the flap down on the side towards his companions, and put his hands in his pockets. "All right," he said, in a slightly altered voice. "When do you go?"

"To-day," answered the Left Bower. "We calculate to take a moonlight pasear over to the Cross Roads and meet the down stage at about twelve to-night. There's plenty of time yet," he added, with a slight laugh; "it's only three o'clock now."

There was a dead silence. Even the rain withheld its continuous patter, a dumb, gray film covered the ashes of the hushed hearth. For the first time the Right Bower exhibited some slight embarrassment.

"I reckon it's held up for a spell," he said, ostentatiously examining the weather, "and we might as well take a run round the claim to see if we've forgotten nothing. Of course, we'll be back again," he added hastily, without looking at the Old Man, "before we go, you know."

The others began to look for their hats, but so awkwardly and with such evident preoccupation of mind that it was not at first discovered that the Judge had his already on. This raised a laugh, as did also a clumsy stumble of Union Mills against the pork barrel, although that gentleman took refuge from his confusion and secured a decent retreat by a gross exaggeration of his lameness, as he limped after the Right Bower. The Judge whistled feebly. The Left Bower, in a more ambitious effort to impart a certain gayety to his exit, stopped on the threshold and said, as if in arch confidence to his companions, "Darned if the Old Man don't look two inches higher since he became a proprietor," laughed patronizingly, and vanished.

If the newly-made proprietor had increased in stature, he had not otherwise changed his demeanor. He remained in the same attitude until the last figure disappeared behind the fringe of buckeye that hid the distant highway. Then he walked slowly to the fire-place, and, leaning against the chimney, kicked the dying embers together with his foot. Something dropped and spattered in the film of hot ashes. Surely the rain had not yet ceased!

His high color had already fled except for a spot on either cheekbone that lent a brightness to his eyes. He glanced around the cabin. It looked familiar and yet strange. Rather, it looked strange BECAUSE still familiar, and therefore incongruous with the new atmosphere that surrounded it—discordant with the echo of their last meeting, and painfully accenting the change. There were the four "bunks," or sleeping berths, of his companions, each still bearing some traces of the individuality of its late occupant with a dumb loyalty that seemed to make their light-hearted defection monstrous. In the dead ashes of the Judge's pipe, scattered on his shelf, still lived his old fire; in the whittled and carved edges of the Left Bower's bunk still were the memories of bygone days of delicious indolence; in the bullet-holes clustered round a knot of one of the beams there was still the record of the Right Bower's old-time skill and practice; in the few engravings of female loveliness stuck upon each headboard there were the proofs of their old extravagant devotion—all a mute protest to the change.

He remembered how, a fatherless, truant schoolboy, he had drifted into their adventurous, nomadic life, itself a life of grown-up truancy like his own, and became one of that gypsy family. How they had taken the place of relations and household in his boyish fancy, filling it with the unsubstantial pageantry of a child's play at grown-up existence, he knew only too well. But how, from being a pet and protege, he had gradually and unconsciously asserted his own individuality and taken upon his younger shoulders not only a poet's keen appreciation of that life, but its actual responsibilities and half-childish burdens, he never suspected. He had fondly believed that he was a neophyte in their ways, a novice in their charming faith and indolent creed, and they had encouraged it; now their renunciation of that faith could only be an excuse for a renunciation of HIM. The poetry that had for two years invested the material and sometimes even mean details of their existence was too much a part of himself to be lightly dispelled. The lesson of those ingenuous moralists failed, as such lessons are apt to fail; their discipline provoked but did not subdue; a rising indignation, stirred by a sense of injury, mounted to his cheek and eyes. It was slow to come, but was none the less violent that it had been preceded by the benumbing shock of shame and pride.

I hope I shall not prejudice the reader's sympathies if my duty as a simple chronicler compels me to state, therefore, that the sober second thought of this gentle poet was to burn down the cabin on the spot with all its contents. This yielded to a milder counsel—waiting for the return of the party, challenging the Right Bower, a duel to the death, perhaps himself the victim, with a crushing explanation in extremis, "It seems we are ONE too many. No matter; it is settled now. Farewell!" Dimly remembering, however, that there was something of this in the last well-worn novel they had read together, and that his antagonist might recognize it, or even worse, anticipate it himself, the idea was quickly rejected. Besides, the opportunity for an apotheosis of self-sacrifice was past. Nothing remained now but to refuse the proffered bribe of claim and cabin by letter, for he must not wait their return. He tore a leaf from a blotted diary, begun and abandoned long since, and essayed to write. Scrawl after scrawl was torn up, until his fury had cooled down to a frigid third personality. "Mr. John Ford regrets to inform his late partners that their tender of house, of furniture," however, seemed too inconsistent with the pork-barrel table he was writing on; a more eloquent renunciation of their offer became frivolous and idiotic from a caricature of Union Mills, label and all, that appeared suddenly on the other side of the leaf; and when he at last indited a satisfactory and impassioned exposition of his feelings, the legible addendum of "Oh, ain't you glad you're out of the wilderness!"—the forgotten first line of a popular song, which no scratching would erase—seemed too like an ironical postscript to be thought of for a moment. He threw aside his pen and cast the discordant record of past foolish pastime into the dead ashes of the hearth.

How quiet it was. With the cessation of the rain the wind too had gone down, and scarcely a breath of air came through the open door. He walked to the threshold and gazed on the hushed prospect. In this listless attitude he was faintly conscious of a distant reverberation, a mere phantom of sound—perhaps the explosion of a distant blast in the hills—that left the silence more marked and oppressive. As he turned again into the cabin a change seemed to have come over it. It already looked old and decayed. The loneliness of years of desertion seemed to have taken possession of it; the atmosphere of dry rot was in the beams and rafters. To his excited fancy the few disordered blankets and articles of clothing seemed dropping to pieces; in one of the bunks there was a hideous resemblance in the longitudinal heap of clothing to a withered and mummied corpse. So it might look in after years when some passing stranger—but he stopped. A dread of the place was beginning to creep over him; a dread of the days to come, when the monotonous sunshine should lay bare the loneliness of these walls; the long, long days of endless blue and cloudless, overhanging solitude; summer days when the wearying, incessant trade winds should sing around that empty shell and voice its desolation. He gathered together hastily a few articles that were especially his own—rather that the free communion of the camp, from indifference or accident, had left wholly to him. He hesitated for a moment over his rifle, but, scrupulous in his wounded pride, turned away and left the familiar weapon that in the dark days had so often provided the dinner or breakfast of the little household. Candor compels me to state that his equipment was not large nor eminently practical. His scant pack was a light weight for even his young shoulders, but I fear he thought more of getting away from the Past than providing for the Future.

With this vague but sole purpose he left the cabin, and almost mechanically turned his steps towards the creek he had crossed that morning. He knew that by this route he would avoid meeting his companions; its difficulties and circuitousness would exercise his feverish limbs and give him time for reflection. He had determined to leave the claim, but whence he had not yet considered. He reached the bank of the creek where he had stood two hours before; it seemed to him two years. He looked curiously at his reflection in one of the broad pools of overflow, and fancied he looked older. He watched the rush and outset of the turbid current hurrying to meet the South Fork, and to eventually lose itself in the yellow Sacramento. Even in his preoccupation he was impressed with a likeness to himself and his companions in this flood that had burst its peaceful boundaries. In the drifting fragments of one of their forgotten flumes washed from the bank, he fancied he saw an omen of the disintegration and decay of the Lone Star claim.

The strange hush in the air that he had noticed before—a calm so inconsistent with that hour and the season as to seem portentous— became more marked in contrast to the feverish rush of the turbulent water-course. A few clouds lazily huddled in the west apparently had gone to rest with the sun on beds of somnolent poppies. There was a gleam as of golden water everywhere along the horizon, washing out the cold snowpeaks, and drowning even the rising moon. The creek caught it here and there, until, in grim irony, it seemed to bear their broken sluice-boxes and useless engines on the very Pactolian stream they had been hopefully created to direct and carry. But by some peculiar trick of the atmosphere, the perfect plenitude of that golden sunset glory was lavished on the rugged sides and tangled crest of the Lone Star Mountain. That isolated peak, the landmark of their claim, the gaunt monument of their folly, transfigured in the evening splendor, kept its radiance unquenched long after the glow had fallen from the encompassing skies, and when at last the rising moon, step by step, put out the fires along the winding valley and plains, and crept up the bosky sides of the canyon, the vanishing sunset was lost only to reappear as a golden crown.

The eyes of the young man were fixed upon it with more than a momentary picturesque interest. It had been the favorite ground of his prospecting exploits, its lowest flank had been scarred in the old enthusiastic days with hydraulic engines, or pierced with shafts, but its central position in the claim and its superior height had always given it a commanding view of the extent of their valley and its approaches, and it was this practical pre-eminence that alone attracted him at that moment. He knew that from its crest he would be able to distinguish the figures of his companions, as they crossed the valley near the cabin, in the growing moonlight. Thus he could avoid encountering them on his way to the high road, and yet see them, perhaps, for the last time. Even in his sense of injury there was a strange satisfaction in the thought.

The ascent was toilsome, but familiar. All along the dim trail he was accompanied by gentler memories of the past, that seemed, like the faint odor of spiced leaves and fragrant grasses wet with the rain and crushed beneath his ascending tread, to exhale the sweeter perfume in his effort to subdue or rise above them. There was the thicket of manzanita, where they had broken noonday bread together; here was the rock beside their maiden shaft, where they had poured a wild libation in boyish enthusiasm of success; and here the ledge where their first flag, a red shirt heroically sacrificed, was displayed from a long-handled shovel to the gaze of admirers below. When he at last reached the summit, the mysterious hush was still in the air, as if in breathless sympathy with his expedition. In the west, the plain was faintly illuminated, but disclosed no moving figures. He turned towards the rising moon, and moved slowly to the eastern edge. Suddenly he stopped. Another step would have been his last! He stood upon the crumbling edge of a precipice. A landslip had taken place on the eastern flank, leaving the gaunt ribs and fleshless bones of Lone Star Mountain bare in the moonlight. He understood now the strange rumble and reverberation he had heard; he understood now the strange hush of bird and beast in brake and thicket!

Although a single rapid glance convinced him that the slide had taken place in an unfrequented part of the mountain, above an inaccessible canyon, and reflection assured him his companions could not have reached that distance when it took place, a feverish impulse led him to descend a few rods in the track of the avalanche. The frequent recurrence of outcrop and angle made this comparatively easy. Here he called aloud; the feeble echo of his own voice seemed only a dull impertinence to the significant silence. He turned to reascend; the furrowed flank of the mountain before him lay full in the moonlight. To his excited fancy, a dozen luminous star-like points in the rocky crevices started into life as he faced them. Throwing his arm over the ledge above him, he supported himself for a moment by what appeared to be a projection of the solid rock. It trembled slightly. As he raised himself to its level, his heart stopped beating. It was simply a fragment detached from the outcrop, lying loosely on the ledge but upholding him by ITS OWN WEIGHT ONLY. He examined it with trembling fingers; the encumbering soil fell from its sides and left its smoothed and worn protuberances glistening in the moonlight. It was virgin gold!

Looking back upon that moment afterwards, he remembered that he was not dazed, dazzled, or startled. It did not come to him as a discovery or an accident, a stroke of chance or a caprice of fortune. He saw it all in that supreme moment; Nature had worked out their poor deduction. What their feeble engines had essayed spasmodically and helplessly against the curtain of soil that hid the treasure, the elements had achieved with mightier but more patient forces. The slow sapping of the winter rains had loosened the soil from the auriferous rock, even while the swollen stream was carrying their impotent and shattered engines to the sea.

What mattered that his single arm could not lift the treasure he had found! What mattered that to unfix those glittering stars would still tax both skill and patience! The work was done, the goal was reached! even his boyish impatience was content with that. He rose slowly to his feet, unstrapped his long-handled shovel from his back, secured it in the crevice, and quietly regained the summit.

It was all his own! His own by right of discovery under the law of the land, and without accepting a favor from THEM. He recalled even the fact that it was HIS prospecting on the mountain that first suggested the existence of gold in the outcrop and the use of the hydraulic. HE had never abandoned that belief, whatever the others had done. He dwelt somewhat indignantly to himself on this circumstance, and half unconsciously faced defiantly towards the plain below. But it was sleeping peacefully in the full sight of the moon, without life or motion. He looked at the stars; it was still far from midnight. His companions had no doubt long since returned to the cabin to prepare for their midnight journey. They were discussing him, perhaps laughing at him, or worse, pitying him and his bargain. Yet here was his bargain! A slight laugh he gave vent to here startled him a little, it sounded so hard and so unmirthful, and so unlike, as he oddly fancied, what he really THOUGHT. But WHAT did he think?

Nothing mean or revengeful; no, they never would say THAT. When he had taken out all the surface gold and put the mine in working order, he would send them each a draft for a thousand dollars. Of course, if they were ever ill or poor he would do more. One of the first, the very first things he should do would be to send them each a handsome gun and tell them that he only asked in return the old-fashioned rifle that once was his. Looking back at the moment in after years, he wondered that, with this exception, he made no plans for his own future, or the way he should dispose of his newly acquired wealth. This was the more singular as it had been the custom of the five partners to lie awake at night, audibly comparing with each other what they would do in case they made a strike. He remembered how, Alnaschar-like, they nearly separated once over a difference in the disposal of a hundred thousand dollars that they never had, nor expected to have. He remembered how Union Mills always began his career as a millionnaire by a "square meal" at Delmonico's; how the Right Bower's initial step was always a trip home "to see his mother"; how the Left Bower would immediately placate the parents of his beloved with priceless gifts (it may be parenthetically remarked that the parents and the beloved one were as hypothetical as the fortune); and how the

Judge would make his first start as a capitalist by breaking a certain faro bank in Sacramento. He himself had been equally eloquent in extravagant fancy in those penniless days, he who now was quite cold and impassive beside the more extravagant reality.

How different it might have been! If they had only waited a day longer! if they had only broken their resolves to him kindly and parted in good will! How he would long ere this have rushed to greet them with the joyful news! How they would have danced around it, sung themselves hoarse, laughed down their enemies, and run up the flag triumphantly on the summit of the Lone Star Mountain! How they would have crowned him "the Old Man," "the hero of the camp!" How he would have told them the whole story; how some strange instinct had impelled him to ascend the summit, and how another step on that summit would have precipitated him into the canyon! And how—but what if somebody else, Union Mills or the Judge, had been the first discoverer? Might they not have meanly kept the secret from him; have selfishly helped themselves and done—

"What YOU are doing now."

The hot blood rushed to his cheek, as if a strange voice were at his ear. For a moment he could not believe that it came from his own pale lips until he found himself speaking. He rose to his feet, tingling with shame, and began hurriedly to descend the mountain.

He would go to them, tell them of his discovery, let them give him his share, and leave them forever. It was the only thing to be done, strange that he had not thought of it at once. Yet it was hard, very hard and cruel to be forced to meet them again. What had he done to suffer this mortification? For a moment he actually hated this vulgar treasure that had forever buried under its gross ponderability the light and careless past, and utterly crushed out the poetry of their old, indolent, happy existence.

He was sure to find them waiting at the Cross Roads where the coach came past. It was three miles away, yet he could get there in time if he hastened. It was a wise and practical conclusion of his evening's work, a lame and impotent conclusion to his evening's indignation. No matter. They would perhaps at first think he had come to weakly follow them, perhaps they would at first doubt his story. No matter. He bit his lips to keep down the foolish rising tears, but still went blindly forward.

He saw not the beautiful night, cradled in the dark hills, swathed in luminous mists, and hushed in the awe of its own loveliness! Here and there the moon had laid her calm face on lake and overflow, and gone to sleep embracing them, until the whole plain seemed to be lifted into infinite quiet. Walking on as in a dream, the black, impenetrable barriers of skirting thickets opened and gave way to vague distances that it appeared impossible to reach, dim vistas that seemed unapproachable. Gradually he seemed himself to become a part of the mysterious night. He was becoming as pulseless, as calm, as passionless.

What was that? A shot in the direction of the cabin! yet so faint, so echoless, so ineffective in the vast silence, that he would have thought it his fancy but for the strange instinctive jar upon his sensitive nerves. Was it an accident, or was it an intentional signal to him? He stopped; it was not repeated, the silence reasserted itself, but this time with an ominous death-like suggestion. A sudden and terrible thought crossed his mind. He cast aside his pack and all encumbering weight, took a deep breath, lowered his head and darted like a deer in the direction of the challenge.

~~~~~~

The exodus of the seceding partners of the Lone Star claim had been scarcely an imposing one. For the first five minutes after quitting the cabin, the procession was straggling and vagabond. Unwonted exertion had exaggerated the lameness of some, and feebleness of moral purpose had predisposed the others to obtrusive musical exhibition. Union Mills limped and whistled with affected abstraction; the Judge whistled and limped with affected earnestness. The Right Bower led the way with some show of definite design; the Left Bower followed with his hands in his pockets. The two feebler natures, drawn together in unconscious sympathy, looked vaguely at each other for support.

"You see," said the Judge, suddenly, as if triumphantly concluding an argument, "there ain't anything better for a young fellow than independence. Nature, so to speak, points the way. Look at the animals."

"There's a skunk hereabouts," said Union Mills, who was supposed to be gifted with aristocratically sensitive nostrils, "within ten miles of this place; like as not crossing the Ridge. It's always my luck to happen out just at such times. I don't see the necessity anyhow of trapesing round the claim now, if we calculate to leave it to-night."

Both men waited to observe if the suggestion was taken up by the Right and Left Bower moodily plodding ahead. No response following, the Judge shamelessly abandoned his companion.

"You wouldn't stand snoopin' round instead of lettin' the Old Man get used to the idea alone? No; I could see all along that he was takin' it in, takin' it in, kindly but slowly, and I reckoned the best thing for us to do was to git up and git until he'd got round it." The Judge's voice was slightly raised for the benefit of the two before him.

"Didn't he say," remarked the Right Bower, stopping suddenly and facing the others, "didn't he say that that new trader was goin' to let him have some provisions anyway?"

Union Mills turned appealingly to the Judge; that gentleman was forced to reply, "Yes; I remember distinctly he said it. It was one of the things I was particular about on his account," responded the Judge, with the air of having arranged it all himself with the new trader. "I remember I was easier in my mind about it."

"But didn't he say," queried the Left Bower, also stopping short, "suthin' about it's being contingent on our doing some work on the race?"

The Judge turned for support to Union Mills, who, however, under the hollow pretense of preparing for a long conference, had luxuriously seated himself on a stump. The Judge sat down also, and replied, hesitatingly, "Well, yes! Us or him."

"Us or him," repeated the Right Bower, with gloomy irony. "And you ain't quite clear in your mind, are you, if YOU haven't done the work already? You're just killing yourself with this spontaneous, promiscuous, and premature overwork; that's what's the matter with you."

"I reckon I heard somebody say suthin' about it's being a Chinaman's three-day job," interpolated the Left Bower, with equal irony, "but I ain't quite clear in my mind about that."

"It'll be a sorter distraction for the Old Man," said Union Mills, feebly—"kinder take his mind off his loneliness."

Nobody taking the least notice of the remark, Union Mills stretched out his legs more comfortably and took out his pipe. He had scarcely done so when the Right Bower, wheeling suddenly, set off in the direction of the creek. The Left Bower, after a slight pause, followed without a word. The Judge, wisely conceiving it better to join the stronger party, ran feebly after him, and left Union Mills to bring up a weak and vacillating rear.

Their course, diverging from Lone Star Mountain, led them now directly to the bend of the creek, the base of their old ineffectual operations. Here was the beginning of the famous tail-race that skirted the new trader's claim, and then lost its way in a swampy hollow. It was choked with debris; a thin, yellow stream that once ran through it seemed to have stopped work when they did, and gone into greenish liquidation.

They had scarcely spoken during this brief journey, and had received no other explanation from the Right Bower, who led them, than that afforded by his mute example when he reached the race. Leaping into it without a word, he at once began to clear away the broken timbers and driftwood. Fired by the spectacle of what appeared to be a new and utterly frivolous game, the men gayly leaped after him, and were soon engaged in a fascinating struggle with the impeded race. The Judge forgot his lameness in springing over a broken sluice-box; Union Mills forgot his whistle in a happy imitation of a Chinese coolie's song. Nevertheless, after ten minutes of this mild dissipation, the pastime flagged; Union Mills was beginning to rub his leg when a distant rumble shook the earth. The men looked at each other; the diversion was complete; a languid discussion of the probabilities of its being an earthquake or a blast followed, in the midst of which the Right Bower, who was working a little in advance of the others, uttered a warning cry and leaped from the race. His companions had barely time to follow before a sudden and inexplicable rise in the waters of the creek sent a swift irruption of the flood through the race. In an instant its choked and impeded channel was cleared, the race was free, and the scattered debris of logs and timber floated upon its easy current. Quick to take advantage of this labor-saving phenomenon, the Lone Star partners sprang into the water, and by disentangling and directing the eddying fragments completed their work.

"The Old Man oughter been here to see this," said the Left Bower; "it's just one o' them climaxes of poetic justice he's always huntin' up. It's easy to see what's happened. One o' them high-toned shrimps over in the Excelsior claim has put a blast in too near the creek. He's tumbled the bank into the creek and sent the back water down here just to wash out our race. That's what I call poetical retribution."

"And who was it advised us to dam the creek below the race and make it do the thing?" asked the Right Bower, moodily.

"That was one of the Old Man's ideas, I reckon," said the Left Bower, dubiously.

"And you remember," broke in the Judge with animation, "I allus said, 'Go slow, go slow. You just hold on and suthin' will happen.' And," he added, triumphantly, "you see suthin' has happened. I don't want to take credit to myself, but I reckoned on them Excelsior boys bein' fools, and took the chances."

"And what if I happen to know that the Excelsior boys ain't blastin' to-day?" said the Right Bower, sarcastically.

As the Judge had evidently based his hypothesis on the alleged fact of a blast, he deftly evaded the point. "I ain't saying the Old Man's head ain't level on some things; he wants a little more sabe of the world. He's improved a good deal in euchre lately, and in poker—well! he's got that sorter dreamy, listenin'-to-the-angels kind o' way that you can't exactly tell whether he's bluffin' or has got a full hand. Hasn't he?" he asked, appealing to Union Mills.

But that gentleman, who had been watching the dark face of the Right Bower, preferred to take what he believed to be his cue from him. "That ain't the question," he said virtuously; "we ain't takin' this step to make a card sharp out of him. We're not doin' Chinamen's work in this race to-day for that. No, sir! We're teachin' him to paddle his own canoe." Not finding the sympathetic response he looked for in the Right Bower's face, he turned to the Left.

"I reckon we were teachin' him our canoe was too full," was the Left Bower's unexpected reply. "That's about the size of it."

The Right Bower shot a rapid glance under his brows at his brother. The latter, with his hands in his pockets, stared unconsciously at the rushing waters, and then quietly turned away. The Right Bower followed him. "Are you goin' back on us?" he asked.

"Are you?" responded the other.

"No!"

"NO, then it is," returned the Left Bower quietly. The elder brother hesitated in half-angry embarrassment.

"Then what did you mean by saying we reckoned our canoe was too full?"

"Wasn't that our idea?" returned the Left Bower, indifferently.

Confounded by this practical expression of his own unformulated good intentions, the Right Bower was staggered.

"Speakin' of the Old Man," broke in the Judge, with characteristic infelicity, "I reckon he'll sort o' miss us, times like these. We were allers runnin' him and bedevilin' him, after work, just to get him excited and amusin', and he'll kinder miss that sort o' stimulatin'. I reckon we'll miss it too, somewhat. Don't you remember, boys, the night we put up that little sell on him and made him believe we'd struck it rich in the bank of the creek, and got him so conceited, he wanted to go off and settle all our debts at once?"

"And how I came bustin' into the cabin with a pan full of iron pyrites and black sand," chuckled Union Mills, continuing the reminiscences, "and how them big gray eyes of his nearly bulged out of his head. Well, it's some satisfaction to know we did our duty by the young fellow even in those little things." He turned for confirmation of their general disinterestedness to the Right Bower, but he was already striding away, uneasily conscious of the lazy following of the Left Bower, like a laggard conscience at his back. This movement again threw

Union Mills and the Judge into feeble complicity in the rear, as the procession slowly straggled homeward from the creek.

Night had fallen. Their way lay through the shadow of Lone Star Mountain, deepened here and there by the slight, bosky ridges that, starting from its base, crept across the plain like vast roots of its swelling trunk. The shadows were growing blacker as the moon began to assert itself over the rest of the valley, when the Right Bower halted suddenly on one of these ridges. The Left Bower lounged up to him, and stopped also, while the two others came up and completed the group.

"There's no light in the shanty," said the Right Bower in a low voice, half to himself, and half in answer to their inquiring attitude. The men followed the direction of his finger. In the distance the black outline of the Lone Star cabin stood out distinctly in the illumined space. There was the blank, sightless, external glitter of moonlight on its two windows that seemed to reflect its dim vacancy, empty alike of light, and warmth, and motion.

"That's sing'lar," said the Judge in an awed whisper.

The Left Bower, by simply altering the position of his hands in his trousers' pockets, managed to suggest that he knew perfectly the meaning of it, had always known it; but that being now, so to speak, in the hands of Fate, he was callous to it. This much, at least, the elder brother read in his attitude. But anxiety at that moment was the controlling impulse of the Right Bower, as a certain superstitious remorse was the instinct of the two others, and without heeding the cynic, the three started at a rapid pace for the cabin.

They reached it silently, as the moon, now riding high in the heavens, seemed to touch it with the tender grace and hushed repose of a tomb. It was with something of this feeling that the Right Bower softly pushed open the door; it was with something of this dread that the two others lingered on the threshold, until the Right Bower, after vainly trying to stir the dead embers on the hearth into life with his foot, struck a match and lit their solitary candle. Its flickering light revealed the familiar interior unchanged in aught but one thing. The bunk that the Old Man had occupied was stripped of its blankets; the few cheap ornaments and photographs were gone; the rude poverty of the bare boards and scant pallet looked up at them unrelieved by the bright face and gracious youth that had once made them tolerable. In the grim irony of that exposure, their own penury was doubly conscious. The little knapsack, the teacup and coffee-pot that had hung near his bed, were gone also. The most indignant protest, the most pathetic of the letters he had composed and rejected, whose torn fragments still littered the floor, could never have spoken with the eloquence of this empty space! The men exchanged no words: the solitude of the cabin, instead of drawing them together, seemed to isolate each one in selfish distrust of the others. Even the unthinking garrulity of Union Mills and the Judge was checked. A moment later, when the Left Bower entered the cabin, his presence was scarcely noticed.

The silence was broken by a joyous exclamation from the Judge. He had discovered the Old Man's rifle in the corner, where it had been at first overlooked. "He ain't gone yet, gentlemen—for yer's his rifle," he broke in, with a feverish return of volubility, and a high excited falsetto. "He wouldn't have left this behind. No! I knowed it from the first. He's just outside a bit, foraging for wood and water. No, sir! Coming along here I said to Union Mills—didn't I?—'Bet your life the Old Man's not far off, even if he ain't in the cabin.' Why, the moment I stepped foot—"

"And I said coming along," interrupted Union Mills, with equally reviving mendacity. "Like as not he's hangin' round yer and lyin' low just to give us a surprise. He! ho!"

"He's gone for good, and he left that rifle here on purpose," said the Left Bower in a low voice, taking the weapon almost tenderly in his hands.

"Drop it, then!" said the Right Bower. The voice was that of his brother, but suddenly changed with passion. The two other partners instinctively drew back in alarm.

"I'll not leave it here for the first comer," said the Left Bower, calmly, "because we've been fools and he too. It's too good a weapon for that."

"Drop it, I say!" said the Right Bower, with a savage stride towards him.

The younger brother brought the rifle to a half charge with a white face but a steady eye.

"Stop where you are!" he said collectedly. "Don't row with ME, because you haven't either the grit to stick to your ideas or the heart to confess them wrong. We've followed your lead, and—here we are! The camp's broken up—the Old Man's gone—and we're going. And as for the d----d rifle—"

"Drop it, do you hear!" shouted the Right Bower, clinging to that one idea with the blind pertinacity of rage and a losing cause. "Drop it!"

The Left Bower drew back, but his brother had seized the barrel with both hands. There was a momentary struggle, a flash through the half-lighted cabin, and a shattering report. The two men fell back from each other; the rifle dropped on the floor between them.

The whole thing was over so quickly that the other two partners had not had time to obey their common impulse to separate them, and consequently even now could scarcely understand what had passed. It was over so quickly that the two actors themselves walked back to their places, scarcely realizing their own act.

A dead silence followed. The Judge and Union Mills looked at each other in dazed astonishment, and then nervously set about their former habits, apparently in that fatuous belief common to such natures, that they were ignoring a painful situation. The Judge drew the barrel towards him, picked up the cards, and began mechanically to "make a patience," on which Union Mills gazed with ostentatious interest, but with eyes furtively conscious of the rigid figure of the Right Bower by the chimney and the abstracted face of the Left Bower at the door. Ten minutes had passed in this occupation, the Judge and Union Mills conversing in the furtive whispers of children unavoidably but fascinatedly present at a family quarrel, when a light step was heard upon the crackling brushwood outside, and the bright panting face of the Old Man appeared upon the threshold. There was a shout of joy; in another moment he was half-buried in the bosom of the Right Bower's shirt, half-dragged into the lap of the Judge, upsetting the barrel, and completely encompassed by the Left Bower and Union Mills. With the enthusiastic utterance of his name the spell was broken.

Happily unconscious of the previous excitement that had provoked this spontaneous unanimity of greeting, the Old Man, equally relieved, at once broke into a feverish announcement of his discovery. He painted the details, with, I fear, a slight exaggeration of coloring, due partly to his own excitement, and partly to justify their own. But he was strangely conscious that these bankrupt men appeared less elated with their personal interest in their stroke of fortune than with his own success. "I told you he'd do it," said the Judge, with a reckless unscrupulousness of statement that carried everybody with it; "look at him! the game little pup." "Oh no! he ain't the right breed, is he?" echoed Union Mills with arch irony, while the Right and Left Bower, grasping either hand, pressed a proud but silent greeting that was half new to him, but wholly delicious. It was not without difficulty that he could at last prevail upon them to return with him to the scene of his discovery, or even then restrain them from attempting to carry him thither on their shoulders on the plea of his previous prolonged exertions. Once only there was a momentary embarrassment. "Then you fired that shot to bring me back?" said the Old Man, gratefully. In the awkward silence that followed, the hands of the two brothers sought and grasped each other, penitently. "Yes," interposed the Judge, with delicate tact, "ye see the Right and Left Bower almost quarreled to see which should be the first to fire for ye. I disremember which did"—"I never touched the trigger," said the Left Bower, hastily. With a hurried backward kick, the Judge resumed, "It went off sorter spontaneous."

The difference in the sentiment of the procession that once more issued from the Lone Star cabin did not fail to show itself in each individual partner according to his temperament. The subtle tact of Union Mills, however, in expressing an awakened respect for their fortunate partner by addressing him, as if unconsciously, as "Mr. Ford" was at first discomposing, but even this was forgotten in their breathless excitement as they neared the base of the mountain. When they had crossed the creek the Right Bower stopped reflectively.

"You say you heard the slide come down before you left the cabin?" he said, turning to the Old Man.

"Yes; but I did not know then what it was. It was about an hour and a half after you left," was the reply.

"Then look here, boys," continued the Right Bower with superstitious exultation; "it was the SLIDE that tumbled into the creek, overflowed it, and helped US clear out the race!"

It seemed so clear that Providence had taken the partners of the Lone Star directly in hand that they faced the toilsome ascent of the mountain with the assurance of conquerors. They paused only on the summit to allow the Old Man to lead the way to the slope that held their treasure. He advanced cautiously to the edge of the crumbling cliff, stopped, looked bewildered, advanced again, and then remained white and immovable. In an instant the Right Bower was at his side.

"Is anything the matter? Don't—don't look so, Old Man, for God's sake!"

The Old Man pointed to the dull, smooth, black side of the mountain, without a crag, break, or protuberance, and said with ashen lips:

"It's gone!"

And it was gone! A SECOND slide had taken place, stripping the flank of the mountain, and burying the treasure and the weak implement that had marked its side deep under a chaos of rock and debris at its base.

"Thank God!" The blank faces of his companions turned quickly to the Right Bower. "Thank God!" he repeated, with his arm round the neck of the Old Man. "Had he stayed behind he would have been buried too." He paused, and, pointing solemnly to the depths below, said, "And thank God for showing us where we may yet labor for it in hope and patience like honest men."

The men silently bowed their heads and slowly descended the mountain. But when they had reached the plain one of them called out to the others to watch a star that seemed to be rising and moving towards them over the hushed and sleeping valley.

"It's only the stage coach, boys," said the Left Bower, smiling; "the coach that was to take us away."

In the security of their new-found fraternity they resolved to wait and see it pass. As it swept by with flash of light, beat of hoofs, and jingle of harness, the only real presence in the dreamy landscape, the driver shouted a hoarse greeting to the phantom partners, audible only to the Judge, who was nearest the vehicle.

"Did you hear—DID you hear what he said, boys?" he gasped, turning to his companions. "No! Shake hands all round, boys! God bless you all, boys! To think we didn't know it all this while!"

"Know what?"

"Merry Christmas!"

15

THE END OF THE TRAIL

BY HAMLIN GARLAND

There comes a time in any pursuit when reality sets in like a dagger to the heart: The game is over; you lost! Distinguished writer Hamlin Garland puts us on the gold trail into the Klondike and describes facing up to the bitter time when he gave up the chase and headed home.

The next morning we hired a large unpainted skiff and by working very hard ourselves in addition to paying full fare we reached camp at about ten o'clock in the morning. Atlin City was also a clump of tents half hidden in the trees on the beach of the lake near the mouth of Pine Creek. The lake was surpassingly beautiful under the morning sun.

A crowd of sullen, profane, and grimy men were lounging around, cursing the commissioners and the police. The beach was fringed with rowboats and canoes, like a New England fishing village, and all day long men were loading themselves into these boats, hungry, tired, and weary, hastening back to Skagway or the coast; while others, fresh, buoyant, and hopeful, came gliding in.

To those who came, the sullen and disappointed ones who were about to go uttered approbrious cries: "See the damn fools come! What d'you think you're doin'? On a fishin' excursion?"

We went into camp on the water front, and hour after hour men laden with packs tramped ceaselessly to and fro along the pathway just below our door. I was now chief cook and bottle washer, my partner, who was entirely unaccustomed to work of this kind, having the status of a boarder.

The lake was a constant joy to us. As the sun sank the glacial mountains to the southwest became most royal in their robes of purple and silver. The sky filled with crimson and saffron clouds which the lake reflected like a mirror. The little rocky islands drowsed in the mist like some strange monsters sleeping on the bosom of the water. The men were filthy and profane for the most part, and made enjoyment of nature almost impossible. Many of them were of the rudest and most uninteresting types, nomads—almost tramps. They had nothing of the epic qualities which belong to the mountaineers and natural miners of the Rocky Mountains. Many of them were loafers and ne'er-do-wells from Skagway and other towns of the coast.

We had a gold pan, a spade, and a pick. Therefore early the next morning we flung a little pack of grub over our shoulders and set forth to test the claims which were situated upon Pine Creek, a stream which entered Lake Atlin near the camp. It was said to be eighteen miles long and Discovery claim was some eight miles up.

We traced our way up the creek as far as Discovery and back, panning dirt at various places with resulting colors in some cases. The trail was full of men racking to and fro with heavy loads on their backs. They moved in little trains of four or five or six men, some going out of the country, others coming in—about an equal number each way. Everything along the creek was staked, and our test work resulted in nothing more than gaining information with regard to what was going on.

The camps on the hills at night swarmed with men in hot debate. The majority believed the camps to be a failure, and loud discussions resounded from the trees as partner and I sat at supper. The town-site men were very nervous. The camps were decreasing in population, and the tone was one of general foreboding.

The campfires flamed all along the lake walk, and the talk of each group could be overheard by any one who listened. Altercations went on with clangorous fury. Almost every party was in division. Some enthusiastic individual had made a find, or had seen some one else who had. His cackle reached other groups, and out of the dark hulking figures loomed to listen or to throw in hot missiles of profanity. Phrases multiplied, mingling inextricably.

"Morgan claims thirty cents to the pan . . . good creek claim . . . his sluice is about ready . . . a clean-up last night . . . I don't believe it. . . . No, Sir, I wouldn't give a hundred dollars for the whole damn moose pasture. . . .Well, it's good enough for me. . . . I tell you it's rotten, the whole damn cheese. . . .You've got to stand in with the police or you can't get . . ." and so on and on unendingly, without coherence. I went to sleep only when the sound of the wordy warfare died away.

I permitted myself a day of rest. Borrowing a boat next day, we went out upon the water and up to the mouth of Pine Creek, where we panned some dirt to amuse ourselves. The lake was like liquid glass, the bottom visible at an enormous depth. It made me think of the marvellous water of McDonald Lake in the Kalispels. I steered the boat (with a long-handled spade) and so was able to look about me and absorb at ease the wonderful beauty of this unbroken and unhewn wilderness. The clouds were resplendent, and in every direction the lake vistas were ideally beautiful and constantly changing.

Toward night the sky grew thick and heavy with clouds. The water of the lake was like molten jewels, ruby and amethyst. The boat seemed floating in some strange, ethereal substance hitherto unknown to man—translucent and iridescent. The mountains loomed like dim purple pillars at the western gate of the world, and the rays of the half-hidden sun plunging athwart these sentinels sank deep into the shining flood. Later the sky cleared, and the inverted mountains in the lake were scarcely less vivid than those which rose into the sky.

The next day I spent with gold pan and camera, working my way up Spruce Creek, a branch of Pine. I found men cheerily at work getting out sluice boxes and digging ditches. I panned everywhere, but did not get much in the way of colors, but the creek seemed to grow better as I went up, and promised very rich returns. I came back rushing, making five miles just inside an hour, hungry and tired.

The crowded camp thinned out. The faint-hearted ones who had no courage to sweat for gold sailed away. Others went out upon their claims to build cabins and lay sluices. I found them whip-sawing lumber, building cabins, and digging ditches. Each day the news grew more encouraging, each day brought the discovery of a new creek or a lake. Men came back in swarms and reporting finds on "Lake Surprise," a newly discovered big body of water, and at last came the report of surprising discoveries in the benches high above the creek.

In the camp one night I heard a couple of men talking around a campfire near me. One of them said: "Why, you know old Sperry was digging on the ridge just above Discovery and I came along and see him up there. And I said, 'Hullo, uncle, what you doin', diggin' your grave?' And the old feller said, 'You just wait a few minutes and I'll show ye.' Well, sir, he filled up a sack o' dirt and toted it down to the creek, and I went along with him to see him wash it out, and say, he took $3.25 out of one pan of that dirt, and $1.85 out of the other pan. Well, that knocked me. I says, 'Uncle, you're all right.' And then I made tracks for a bench claim next to him. Well, about that time everybody began to hustle for bench claims, and now you can't get one anywhere near him."

At another camp, a packer was telling of an immense nugget that had been discovered somewhere on the upper waters of Birch Creek. "And say, fellers, you know there is another lake up there pretty near as big as Atlin. They are calling it Lake Surprise. I heard a feller say a few days ago there was a big lake up there and I thought he meant a lake six or eight miles long. On the very high ground next to Birch, you can look down over that lake and I bet it's sixty miles long. It must reach nearly to Teslin Lake." There was something pretty fine in the thought of being in a country where lakes sixty miles long were being discovered and set forth on the maps of the world. Up to this time Atlin Lake itself was unmapped. To an unpractical man like myself it was reward enough to feel the thrill of excitement which comes with such discoveries.

However, I was not a goldseeker, and when I determined to give up any further pursuit of mining and to delegate it entirely to my partner, I experienced a feeling of relief. I determined to "stick to my last," notwithstanding the fascination which I felt in the sight of placer gold. Quartz mining has never had the slightest attraction for me, but to see the gold washed out of the sand, to see it appear bright and shining in the black sand in the bottom of the pan, is really worth while. It is first-hand contact with Nature's stores of wealth.

I went up to Discovery for the last time with my camera slung over my shoulder, and my note-book in hand to take a final survey of the miners and to hear for the last time their exultant talk. I found them exceedingly cheerful, even buoyant.

The men who had gone in with ten days' provisions, the tender-foot miners, the men "with a cigarette and a sandwich," had gone out. Those who remained were men who knew their business and were resolute and self-sustaining.

There was a crowd of such men around the land-office tents and many filings were made. Nearly every man had his little phial of gold to show. No one was loud, but every one seemed to be quietly confident and replied to my questions in a low voice, "Well, you can safely say the country is all right."

The day was fine like September in Wisconsin. The lake as I walked back to it was very alluring. My mind returned again and again to the things I had left behind for so long. My correspondence, my books, my friends, all the literary interests of my life, began to reassert their dominion over me. For some time I had realized that this was almost an ideal spot for camping or mining. Just over in the wild country toward Teslin Lake, herds of caribou were grazing. Moose and bear were being killed daily, rich and unknown streams were waiting for the gold pan, the pick and the shovel, but—it was not for me! I was ready to return—eager to return.

The day on which I crossed the lake to Taku City was most glorious. A September haze lay on the mountains, whose high slopes, orange, ruby, and golden-green, allured with almost irresistible attraction. Although the clouds were gathering in the east, the sunset was superb. Taku arm seemed a river of gold sweeping between gates of purple. As the darkness came on, a long creeping line of fire crept up a near-by mountain's side, and from time to time, as it reached some great pine, it flamed to the clouds like a mighty geyser of red-hot lava. It was splendid but terrible to witness.

The next day was a long, long wait for the steamer. I now had in my pocket just twelve dollars, but possessed a return ticket on one of the boats. This ticket was not good on any other boat, and naturally I felt considerable anxiety for fear it would not turn up. My dinner consisted of moose steak, potatoes, and bread, and was most thoroughly enjoyed.

At last the steamer came, but it was not the one on which I had secured passage, and as it took almost my last dollar to pay for deck passage thereon, I lived on some small cakes of my own baking, which I carried in a bag. I was now in a sad predicament unless I should connect at Lake Bennett with some one who would carry my outfit back to Skagway on credit. I ate my stale cakes and drank lake water, and thus fooled the little Jap steward out of two dollars. It was a sad business, but unavoidable.

The lake being smooth, the trip consumed but thirteen hours, and we arrived at Bennett Lake late at night. Hoisting my bed and luggage to my shoulder, I went up on the side-hill like a stray dog, and made my bed down on the sand beside a cart, near a shack. The wind, cold and damp, swept over the mountains with a roar. I was afraid the owners of the cart might discover me there, and order me to seek a bed elsewhere. Dogs sniffed around me during the night, but on the whole I slept very well. I could feel the sand blowing over me in the wild gusts of wind which relented not in all my stay at Bennett City.

I spent literally the last cent I had on a scanty breakfast, and then, in company with Doctor G. (a fellow prospector), started on my return to the coast over the far-famed Chilcoot Pass.

At 9 a.m. we took the little ferry for the head of Lindernan Lake. The doctor paid my fare. The boat, a wabbly craft, was crowded with returning Klondikers, many of whom were full of importance and talk of their wealth; while others, sick and worn, with a wistful gleam in their eyes, seemed eager to get back to civilization and medical care. There were some women, also, who had made a fortune in dance-houses and were now bound for New York and Paris, where dresses could be had in the latest styles and in any quantities.

My travelling mate, the doctor, was a tall and vigorous man from Winnipeg, accustomed to a plainsman's life, hardy and resolute. He said, "We ought to make Dyea to-day." I said in reply, "Very well, we can try."

It was ten o'clock when we left the little boat and hit the trail, which was thirty miles long, and passed over the summit three thousand six hundred feet above the sea. The doctor's pace was tremendous, and we soon left every one else behind.

I carried my big coat and camera, which hindered me not a little. For the first part of the journey the doctor preceded me, his broad shoulders keeping off the powerful wind and driving mist, which grew thicker as we rose among the ragged cliffs beside a roaring stream.

That walk was a grim experience. Until two o'clock we climbed resolutely along a rough, rocky, and wooded trail, with the heavy mist driving into our faces. The road led up a rugged cañon and over a fairly good wagon road until somewhere about twelve o'clock. Then the foot trail deflected to the left, and climbed sharply over slippery ledges, along banks of ancient snows in which carcasses of horses lay embedded, and across many rushing little streams. The way grew grimmer each step. At last we came to Crater Lake, and from that point on it was a singular and sinister land of grassless crags swathed in mist. Nothing could be seen at this point but a desolate, flat expanse of barren sands over which gray-green streams wandered in confusion, coming from darkness and vanishing in obscurity. Strange shapes showed in the gray dusk of the Crater. It was like a landscape in hell. It seemed to be the end of the earth, where no life had ever been or could long exist.

Across this flat to its farther wall we took our way, facing the roaring wind now heavy with clouds of rain. At last we stood in the mighty notch of the summit, through which the wind rushed as though hurrying to some far-off, deep-hidden vacuum in the world. The peaks of the mountains were lost in clouds out of which water fell in vicious slashes.

The mist set the imagination free. The pinnacles around us were like those which top the Valley of Desolation. We seemed each moment about to plunge into ladderless abysses. Nothing ever imagined by Poe or Doré could be more singular, more sinister, than these summits in such a light, in such a storm. It might serve as the scene for an exiled devil. The picture of Beelzebub perched on one of those gray, dimly seen crags, his form outlined in the mist, would shake the heart. I thought of "Peer Gynt" wandering in the high home of the Trolls. Crags beetled beyond crags, and nothing could be heard but the wild waters roaring in the obscure depths beneath our feet. There was no sky, no level place, no growing thing, no bird or beast—only crates of bones to show where some heartless master had pushed a faithful horse up these terrible heights to his death.

And here—just here in a world of crags and mist—I heard a shout of laughter, and then bursting upon my sight, strong-limbed, erect, and full-bosomed, appeared a girl. Her face was like a rain-wet rose—a splendid, unexpected flower set in this dim and gray and desolate place. Fearlessly she fronted me to ask the way, a laugh upon her lips, her big gray eyes confident of man's chivalry, modest and sincere. I had been so long among rude men and their coarse consorts that this fair woman lit the mist as if with sudden sunshine—just a moment and was gone. There were others with her, but they passed unnoticed. There in the gloom, like a stately pink rose, I set the Girl of the Mist.

Sheep Camp was the end of the worst portion of the trail. I had now crossed both the famed passes, much improved of course. They are no longer dangerous (a woman in good health can cross them easily), but they are grim and grievous ways. They reek of cruelty and every association that is coarse and hard. They possess a peculiar value to me in that they throw into fadeless splendor the wealth, the calm, the golden sunlight which lay upon the proud beauty of Atlin Lake.

The last hours of the trip formed a supreme test of endurance. At Sheep Camp, a wet and desolate shanty town, eight miles from Dyea, we came upon stages just starting over our road. But as they were all open carriages, and we were both wet with perspiration and rain, and hungry and tired, we refused to book passage.

"To ride eight miles in an open wagon would mean a case of pneumonia to me," I said.

"Quite right," said the doctor, and we pulled out down the road at a smart clip.

The rain had ceased, but the air was raw and the sky gray, and I was very tired, and those eight miles stretched out like a rubber string. Night fell before we had passed over half the road, which lay for the most part down the flat along the Chilcoot River. In fact, we crossed this stream again and again. In places there were bridges, but most of the crossings were fords where it was necessary to wade through the icy water above our shoe tops. Our legs, numb and weary, threw off this chill with greater pain each time. As the night fell we could only see the footpath by the dim shine of its surface patted smooth by the moccasined feet of the Indian packers. At last I walked with a sort of mechanical action which was dependent on my subconscious will. There was nothing else to do but to go through. The doctor was a better walker than I. His long legs had more reach as well as greater endurance. Nevertheless he admitted being about as tired as ever in his life.

At last, when it seemed as though I could not wade any more of those icy streams and continue to walk, we came in sight of the electric lights on the wharfs of Dyea, sparkling like jewels against the gray night. Their radiant promise helped over the last mile miraculously. We were wet to the knees and covered with mud as we entered upon the straggling street of the decaying town. We stopped in at the first restaurant to get something hot to eat, but found ourselves almost too tired to enjoy even pea soup. But it warmed us up a little, and keeping on down the street we came at last to a hotel of very comfortable accommodations. We ordered a fire built to dry our clothing, and staggered up the stairs.

That ended the goldseekers' trail for me. Henceforward I intended to ride—nevertheless I was pleased to think I could still walk thirty miles in eleven hours through a rain storm, and over a summit three thousand six hundred feet in height. The city had not entirely eaten the heart out of my body.

We arose from a dreamless sleep, somewhat sore, but in amazingly good trim considering our condition the night before, and made our way into our muddy clothing with grim resolution. After breakfast we took a small steamer which ran to Skagway, where we spent the day arranging to take the steamer to the south. We felt quite at home in Skagway now, and Chicago seemed not very far away. Having made connection with my bankers I stretched out in my twenty-five cent bunk with the assurance of a gold king.

Here the long trail took a turn. I had been among the miners and hunters for four months. I had been one of them. I had lived the essentials of their lives, and had been able to catch from them some hint of their outlook on life. They were a disappointment to me in some ways. They seemed like mechanisms. They moved as if drawn by some great magnet whose centre was Dawson City. They appeared to drift on and in toward that human maelstrom going irresolutely to their ruin. They did not seem to me strong men—on the contrary, they seemed weak men—or men strong with one insane purpose. They set their faces toward the golden north, and went on and on through every obstacle like men dreaming, like somnambulists—bending their backs to the most crushing burdens, their faces distorted with effort. "On to Dawson!" "To the Klondike!" That was all they knew.

I overtook them in the Fraser River Valley, I found them in Hazleton. They were setting sail at Bennett, tugging oars on the Hotalinqua, and hundreds of them were landing every day at Dawson, there to stand with lax jaws waiting for something to turn up—lost among thousands of their kind swarming in with the same insane purpose.

Skagway was to me a sad place. On either side rose green mountains covered with crawling glaciers. Between these stern walls, a cold and violent wind roared ceaselessly from the sea gates through which the ships drive hurriedly. All these grim presences depressed me. I longed for release from them. I waited with impatience the coming of the steamer which was to rescue me from the merciless beach.

At last it came, and its hoarse boom thrilled the heart of many a homesick man like myself. We had not much to put aboard, and when I climbed the gang-plank it was with a feeling of fortunate escape.

SOURCES

"All Gold Canyon," by Jack London, from *Moon Face and Other Stories*, 1906

"The Lure of Buried Treasure," by Ralph D. Paine, from *The Book of Buried Treasure*, 1911

"The Spell of the Yukon," by Robert W. Service, from *The Spell of the Yukon and Other Verses*, 1907

"Gold and Grizzlies," by Frona Eunice Wait, from *The Stories of El Dorado*, 1904

"Young Treasure Hunters: Huck Finn and Tom Sawyer," by Mark Twain, from *The Adventures of Tom Sawyer*, 1876

"Bad Start at Dawson," by W. H. P. Jarvis, from *The Great Gold Rush*, 1913

"To Build a Fire," by Jack London, from *Lost Face*, 1910

"Treasure Island," by Robert Lewis Stevenson, from the book *Treasure Island*, 1883

"California Gold Rush," by Captain F. S. Bereton, from In*dian and Scout: A Tale of the Great Gold Rush to California*, 1905

"Striking It Rich," by James Oliver Curwood, from *The Gold Hunters*, 1909

"Storm and Stress," by W. H. P. Jarvis, from *The Great Gold Rush*, 1913

"The Pocket Hunter," by Mary Austin, from *The Land of Little Rain*, 1901

"The North Wind's Malice," by Rex Beach, from *Laughing Bill Hyde and Other Stories*, 1917

"Left Out on Lone Star Mountain," by Bret Harte, from *Frontier Stories*, 1887

"The End of the Trail," by Hamlin Garland, from *The Trail of the Gold-seekers*, 1899

CPSIA information can be obtained
at www.ICGtesting.com
Printed in the USA
BVHW030120190921
616994BV00004B/4